YORK NOTE

York Notes Rapid Revision

The Merchant of Venice

AQA GCSE English Literature

Written by Mike Gould

The right of Mike Gould to be identified as the Author of this Work
has been asserted by him in accordance with the Copyright, Designs
and Patents Act 1988

YORK PRESS
322 Old Brompton Road, London SW5 9JH

PEARSON EDUCATION LIMITED
80 Strand, London, WC2R 0RL

10 9 8 7 6 5 4 3 2 1

ISBN 978–1–2922–7100–2

Phototypeset by Carnegie Book Production
Printed in Slovakia

Photo credits:
Lukasz Janyst/Shutterstock for page 4 top / 1000 Words/Shutterstock for page 6 top
and page 30 middle / maradon 333/Shutterstock for page 8 middle and page 34 middle
/ Ukki Studio/Shutterstock for page 10 middle / INTERFOTO/Alamy for page 12 middle
/ Vibrant Pictures/Alamy for page 14 middle and page 28 middle / davidesandriniph/
Shutterstock for page 16 middle / Dario Lo Presti/Shutterstock for page 18 middle /
Falkovskyi/Shutterstock for page 22 bottom / Andrew Mayovskyy/Shutterstock for page
24 bottom / Texturis/Shutterstock for page 26 top right / Natthapenpis Jindatham/
Shutterstock for page 26 top left / alphaspirit/Shutterstock for page 26 bottom /
PaoloGaetano/© iStock for page 32 middle / Elena Vasilchenko/Shutterstock for page
36 middle top / Holmes Garden Photos/Alamy for page 36 middle bottom / pkline/©
iStock for page 38 middle top / Sundraw Photography/Shutterstock for page 38
middle bottom / AF archive/Alamy for page 40 middle / Robert Fried/Alamy for page
40 bottom / Sergei25/Shutterstock for page 44 middle / Alan Smillie/Shutterstock for
page 46 top / ricardoreitmeyer/© iStock for page 48 bottom / David Lyons/Alamy for
page 50 bottom / Suto Norbert Zsolt/Shutterstock for page 52 top / Cristian Andriana/
Shutterstock for page 54 middle / Belozorova Elena/Shutterstock for page 58 middle /
Ceneri/© iStock for page 60 middle

CONTENTS

Five key things about Act I Scenes 1 and 2

1. We are **introduced** to **Antonio**, the **'merchant'** of the title and his friends, including **Bassanio**, who asks to borrow money to woo a noblewoman called **Portia**.
2. We witness **Antonio's melancholy** and his close **friendship** with **Bassanio**.
3. **Venice** (Scene 1), a place of trade, and **Belmont** (Scene 2) are established as the play's **key locations**.
4. The **casket test** devised by **Portia's dead father** is set up as a key **plot device**.
5. The themes of **trade**, **friendship** and **love**, as well as the issue of **fathers and children** are all introduced.

What happens in Scene 1?

- Antonio, a rich merchant with many ships at sea, is unable to say **'why I am so sad'** when questioned about his low mood by friends Salarino and Solanio.
- Bassanio and his young friend Gratiano enter; Bassanio admits his past faults, but asks his friend Antonio to lend him more money to pay his debts.
- Bassanio explains that he has fallen for a noblewoman, Portia, and believes she feels as he does.
- Antonio has no ready money as all his riches are tied up abroad in his trading ships, but he willingly agrees to help Bassanio raise or borrow money.

What happens in Scene 2?

- At her house in Belmont, Portia discusses her frustrations about finding a husband with her lady-in-waiting, Nerissa.
- Portia's late father has set a test for prospective husbands which involves choosing from three caskets of gold, silver and lead in order to win her.
- Portia humorously lists her suitors (a Neapolitan prince, the County Palatine, a French lord, an English baron, a Scottish lord and the Duke of Saxony's nephew) but remembers Bassanio as being worthy of Nerissa's praise.
- The arrival of a suitor, the Prince of Morocco, is announced.

Five key quotations

1. Character of Antonio: **'I have much ado to know myself'** (I.1.7)
2. Bassanio's friendship with Antonio: **'To you, Antonio,/I owe the most in money and in love'** (I.1.130–1)
3. Foreshadowing the risks of Antonio's sea trade: **'all my fortunes are at sea'** (I.1.177)
4. Venice as a business setting – Antonio: **'Try what my credit can in Venice do'** (I.1.180)
5. Fathers clashing with children – Portia: **'so is the will of a living daughter curbed by the will of a dead father'** (I.2.23–4)

Note it!

There are several 'teasers' in these two scenes which show Shakespeare's ability to engage the audience. For example, we are not told exactly what the test of the three caskets set by Portia's father consists of. Also, Antonio's business being all **'at sea'** raises concerns.

Exam focus

How can I write about the use of chance in the plot? AO1 AO2

You can comment on Antonio's business and the test set by Portia's father.

The idea of risk is central to the plot. Antonio's money is entirely tied up in his ships and cargo which are 'all … at sea'. The phrase has a double meaning – they are literally in danger on the ocean, but this is also an idiom that means feeling lost or out of control. Furthermore, the 'lottery' of the test for Portia's suitors, including Bassanio, suggests people's lives may stand or fall according to fortune.	Topic sentence/point
	Quotation supports point
	Language analysis
	Link to other quotation

Now you try!

Finish this paragraph about Antonio's character. Use one of the quotations from the list.

From his first words in the play, Antonio is presented as someone who struggles emotionally ....

Five key things about Act I Scene 3

1. We encounter the main antagonist of the play, **Shylock**, a Jewish moneylender, for the first time.
2. We find out about the **roots of the hate** and conflict **between Shylock and Antonio**.
3. The central **plot device** of the **'pound of flesh' bond** is introduced.
4. Discussions about the **risky nature of sea trade** and **Shylock's trustworthiness** foreshadow later events.
5. Key themes related to **religious prejudice, trade** and **appearance/reality** are developed.

What happens in Scene 3?

- The scene begins *in media res* with Bassanio and Shylock discussing the terms of the loan of 3000 ducats over three months.
- Shylock expresses doubts about whether Antonio's ventures overseas are safe.
- Antonio and Shylock meet. In an aside, Shylock reveals his hate for Antonio and how he wants revenge for the hurt done to him and the Jewish race.
- Antonio and Shylock argue over the meaning of a biblical story about Jacob, which Shylock uses to justify his way of doing business.
- Shylock gives an impassioned speech about how Antonio has treated him, before finally agreeing to the loan, on the conditions of the bond.

What is the bond that Shylock proposes?

- Shylock agrees to loan the money and not take any interest on it. But he proposes that the bond will be a **'merry sport'** (a sort of game or bit of fun).
- The bond states that if Antonio cannot pay back the money within the set time, Shylock can take exactly a **'pound of flesh'** from any part of Antonio's body.
- Bassanio distrusts Shylock and advises Antonio against accepting the bond.
- However, Antonio willingly agrees, saying that within two months he expects to receive three times as much as the loan from his businesses.

Five key quotations

1. Further foreshadowing by Shylock of risks to Antonio: 'he hath ... other ventures he hath squandered abroad' (I.3.17–19)

2. Shylock's aside on the theme of hate and revenge: 'If I can catch him once upon the hip,/I will feed fat the ancient grudge I bear him.' (I.3.41–2)

3. Shylock on the theme of prejudice: 'You call me misbeliever, cut-throat dog,/And spit upon my Jewish gaberdine' (I.3.106–7)

4. Antonio on Shylock's character: 'The devil can cite Scripture for his purpose.' (I.3.93)

5. Bassanio on the theme of appearance and reality: 'I like not fair terms and a villain's mind.' (I.3.175)

Note it!

Shakespeare keeps up the dramatic pace and tension by switching from Belmont directly into the middle of a negotiation between Shylock and Bassanio. This is an example of *in media res* and not only changes the pace but also immediately establishes Shylock's character.

Exam focus

How can I write about the way Shylock is presented?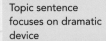

You can comment on Shylock's language and behaviour.

> An aside is a dramatic device often used by Shakespeare to enable his villains to reveal their thoughts or motives. Here, the audience learns that Shylock plans to 'catch' Antonio out to 'feed fat the ancient grudge I bear him.' The image suggests that his hate is very deep-rooted, like an emptiness he must fill. The audience is bound to be anxious for Antonio.

Topic sentence focuses on dramatic device

Quotations support point

Language analysis

Summary point looks forward

Now you try!

Finish this paragraph about Shylock's character. Use one of the quotations from the list.

We are given clues about the danger Shylock poses for Antonio in Bassanio's comment that..

PLOT AND STRUCTURE Act II Scenes 1-5

Five key things about Act II Scenes 1-5

1. We discover more about **the casket test** as the **Prince of Morocco** tries to win Portia's hand.

2. Shylock's daughter **Jessica plans** to run off with **Lorenzo**, a Christian. This is the beginning of another subplot.

3. **Comic characters** are introduced: Shylock's servant **Lancelot** and his father, **Old Gobbo**, who both seek to leave Shylock's house.

4. The theme of **prejudice** is developed in attitudes to Morocco and Shylock.

5. The **theme** of **appearance/reality** is developed through Lancelot and his father, and the plots to deceive Shylock about his daughter's plans.

What happens in Act II Scenes 1-3?

- **Scene 1:** The Prince of Morocco boasts to Portia of his military courage.
- Portia tells him that if he fails the casket test he can never marry.
- **Scene 2:** Shylock's servant, Lancelot, debates with himself about leaving Shylock, and decides he will. He then fools his half-blind father who asks him the way to Shylock's house.
- Bassanio agrees to take Lancelot into his service. He also agrees to take Gratiano to Belmont with him.
- **Scene 3:** Jessica gives Lancelot a letter for her lover, Lorenzo.

How does the subplot develop in Act II Scenes 4 and 5?

- **Scene 4:** Outside Shylock's house, Lorenzo, Gratiano, Salarino and Solanio prepare for a masque.
- Lancelot arrives with the letter inviting Shylock to supper with Bassanio.
- Lorenzo reveals Jessica is to leave her father, taking his **'gold and jewels'**.
- **Scene 5:** Shylock reluctantly goes to meet Bassanio and speaks critically of the **'Christian fools'** who will hold their party close to his house.
- He leaves his keys with Jessica and warns her to **'Lock up'** the doors.

Five key quotations

1. Portia (to Morocco) on the jeopardy of the casket test: **'if you choose wrong,/Never to speak to lady afterward/In way of marriage'** (II.1.40–2)

2. Morocco comments on the theme of prejudice: **'Mislike me not for my complexion'** (II.1.1)

3. Gobbo to Lancelot on the theme of appearance/reality: **'I know you not, young gentleman'** (II.2.65)

4. Jessica on the rift between father and daughter: **'though I am a daughter to his blood/I am not to his manners'** (II.3.17–18)

5. Shylock's scorn: **'I'll go in hate, to feed upon/The prodigal Christian.'** (II.5.14–15)

Note it!

These relatively short scenes introduce urgency and drama, switching swiftly between Belmont and Venice, with plots coming thick and fast. The fact that the audience does not know the outcome of the Prince of Morocco's choice builds further tension.

Exam focus

How can I write about the structure of the action? AO1 AO2

You can comment on the importance of the subplot.

The Lorenzo/Jessica subplot adds weight to Shylock as the antagonist of the play. It is his own daughter, after all, who says that while she may be tied by blood to her father, she cannot put up with 'his manners'. The light-hearted Christians, who include Lorenzo, are thus contrasted with Shylock's instinct to lock up his house and his daughter. Ironically, he leaves her to lock up.

| Topic sentence/point |
| Quotation supports point |
| Explanation and development |
| Summative point about the action |

Now you try!

Finish this paragraph about how prejudice is developed in this act. Use one of the quotations from the list.

The theme of prejudice is developed when Morocco enters the play and his first words to Portia...
....

Five key things about Act II Scenes 6-9

1. **Jessica's elopement** with Lorenzo adds **drama and tension**.
2. Further **details of the casket test** are revealed as two suitors, the Princes of Morocco and Arragon, try to work out the riddles.
3. **Trouble** is foreshadowed with news of ships in danger overseas.
4. The theme of **appearance and reality** is developed through Jessica's disguise, and the way the caskets and inscriptions deceive the princes.
5. The **themes** of **money** and **parental love/duty** are reflected in Shylock's furious response to his daughter Jessica's disappearance.

What happens in Scenes 6 and 7?

- **Scene 6:** Gratiano and Salarino meet Lorenzo. Jessica, disguised as a boy, leaves Shylock's house, taking his money.
- Gratiano leaves to meet Bassanio and get the boat to Belmont.
- **Scene 7:** At Belmont, Morocco reads the three riddle-like inscriptions on the caskets. He is initially attracted by the silver, **'Who chooseth me, shall get as much as he deserves.'**
- He finally opens the gold casket that is inscribed, **'Who chooseth me, shall gain what many men desire'** but is greeted with a skull. He leaves, forlorn.

What happens in Scenes 8 and 9?

- **Scene 8:** Salarino and Solanio report Shylock's angry discovery of Jessica's disappearance.
- They discuss reports of a Venetian ship having sunk in the English Channel and worry it might be Antonio's. They talk of his great love for Bassanio.
- **Scene 9:** At Belmont, Arragon rejects the lead casket, which states, **'Who chooseth me, must give and hazard all he hath'**. He also avoids the trap of the gold casket but vainly believes he deserves Portia, so chooses silver.
- He finds a **'fool's head'** and has to leave. The scene ends with the announcement that Bassanio has arrived.

Five key quotations

1. Jessica on the theme of love: 'love is blind, and lovers cannot see/The pretty follies that themselves commit' (II.6.37–8)

2. Message in the gold casket on the theme of appearance and reality: 'All that glisters is not gold' (II.7.65)

3. Shylock's motive for revenge – Solanio: 'O my Christian ducats!/Justice! The law! My ducats and my daughter!' (II.8.16–17)

4. Foreshadowing of later events by Salarino: 'there miscarried/A vessel of our country richly fraught./I thought upon Antonio' (II.8.30–2)

5. Solanio on Antonio's feelings for Bassanio: 'I think he only loves the world for him.' (II.8.51)

Note it!

The casket test, set by Portia's father, has fairy-tale elements in its structure of three different suitors taking the challenge. The three encounters also touch on key themes of the play: disguise, judgement and justice.

Exam focus

How can I write about the first two casket scenes?

You can comment on the importance of the messages in the caskets.

Although the casket test might seem contrived, the first message is important to the play as a whole. The	Topic sentence/point
phrase, 'All that glisters is not gold' could be seen as	Quotation supports point
a warning to the characters not to make judgements based on outward appearance. Antonio should not	Explanation and development
trust Shylock's seeming 'merry sport'; Shylock should not trust his daughter's apparent loyalty. It leaves the audience wondering – what is true?	Summative point about the theme as a whole

Now you try!

Finish this paragraph about how later plot developments are foreshadowed. Use one of the quotations from the list.

Shakespeare provides hints of Antonio's later difficulties when Salarino...........................

PLOT AND STRUCTURE Act III

Five key things about Act III

1. Rumours about **Antonio's ships** sinking seem to be **confirmed**.
2. **Shylock** resists appeals for **mercy**, and makes it clear he will pursue **payment of his debt** from Antonio in full.
3. **Bassanio** takes the **casket test** and **wins Portia**; **Gratiano** falls for **Nerissa** and they, too, will **marry**.
4. **Bassanio returns to Venice** to help Antonio; **Portia and Nerissa** also leave, in disguise. **Belmont** will be in the hands of **Jessica and Lorenzo**.
5. Themes of **revenge, love, religious prejudice and conflict** are developed.

What happens in Scenes 1-3?

- **Scene 1:** Solanio and Salarino discuss tales of Antonio's lost ship. Shylock arrives and accuses them of knowing about Jessica's flight.

- Shylock gives an impassioned speech about the harm done to him by Antonio. He points out he is as human as any Christian.
- Tubal, Shylock's friend, arrives and makes him even angrier with tales of Jessica's reckless spending of his money.
- **Scene 2:** In Belmont, Bassanio takes the casket test, correctly choosing the lead one and revealing **'Fair Portia's counterfeit'**. Portia gives him a ring as a symbol of their bond.
- A letter arrives confirming Antonio's losses and his imminent death. Bassanio leaves to help him.
- **Scene 3:** Shylock refuses all appeals for mercy; Antonio seems to accept that he is destined to die.

What happens in Scenes 4 and 5?

- **Scene 4:** Back in Belmont, Portia passes management of her house to Jessica and Lorenzo, while she and Nerissa attend a monastery.
- Portia sends a message to a cousin, Doctor Bellario, and reveals to Nerissa they are to go to Venice disguised as young men.
- **Scene 5:** Jessica, Lancelot and Lorenzo talk humorously about parenthood, and about Jessica's conversion to Christianity.

Five key quotations

1. Shylock on prejudice: 'Hath not a Jew eyes? Hath not a Jew hands, organs, dimensions, senses, affections, passions?' (III.1.52–3)
2. Shylock on Jessica's elopement: 'I would my daughter were dead at my foot' (III.1.79)
3. Portia to Bassanio on their relationship: 'Myself, and what is mine, to you and yours/Is now converted.' (III.2.166–7)
4. Dramatic tension – Antonio's losses: 'my ships have all miscarried, my creditors grow cruel' (III.2.313–14)
5. Shylock's relentless character: 'I'll not be made a soft and dull-eyed fool,/To shake the head, relent, and sigh, ... I will have my bond.' (III.3.14–17)

Note it!

After news of Antonio's problems, Portia's playful plan to disguise herself to follow Bassanio may seem out of place, especially as she has recently pledged herself to him. However, it arouses curiosity – why is she doing this?

Exam focus

How can I write about Bassanio winning Portia?

You can comment on how love has social implications.

> In winning Portia, Bassanio is not only gaining the woman he loves, but, ironically given his choice of the lead casket, a lot of wealth. When Portia tells him, 'what is mine, to you and yours/Is now converted' she is referring to all her possessions and lands. Modern audiences might find this hard to accept but this was common practice in Shakespeare's day. However, Shakespeare ensures Portia establishes her independence in other ways.

Topic sentence/point

Quotation supports point

Explanation related to context

Alternative perspective provided

Now you try!

Finish this paragraph about how the news of Antonio's ships builds tension. Use one of the quotations from the list.

As the act opens, Antonio's friends report the possible loss of his ships and, by the end, Antonio confirms this when ....

PLOT AND STRUCTURE Act IV

Five key things about Act IV

1. The act mostly consists of **one long scene** that forms the **dramatic climax** of the play.
2. All the **major characters** are brought into **focus** as the plot nears its end.
3. The **court-room** setting and set-piece **speeches** indicate a **change of mood** and **tone**.
4. **Portia's powerful speech** about **mercy** is the emotional **heart of the scene**.
5. Core themes related to **love**, **friendship**, **justice** and **revenge** intertwine.

What happens at the start of Act IV Scene 1?

- The duke tells Antonio that Shylock is unwilling to show mercy.
- Bassanio offers to pay double the amount he owes to Shylock, but Shylock refuses and prepares to take his bond.
- Nerissa arrives in disguise bearing a letter stating that Balthazar (in fact, Portia) will take the lawyer Dr Bellario's place.

What happens in the second part of Scene 1 and Scene 2?

- **Scene 1:** Portia/Balthazar argues strongly about the importance of mercy, but when Shylock is unmoved, she acknowledges his right to take his **'pound of flesh'**.
- Antonio bares his chest ready for the fatal cut. Suddenly Portia insists no blood must be spilled and explains that if it is, all Shylock's land and goods will pass to the state.
- Shylock is defeated and requests the money, but Portia now tells him that for seeking the life of a Christian he faces execution. The duke pardons him, but Antonio makes him promise to convert to Christianity and leave half his estate to Lorenzo and Jessica.
- Shylock's words as he leaves, **'I am not well'**, show he is now a broken man.
- Portia asks Bassanio for his ring in payment for her service.
- **Scene 2:** Gratiano gives the ring to Portia; Nerissa says she is going to try the same trick on Gratiano to get her engagement ring back.

Five key quotations

1. Antonio on Shylock's vengeful character: **'You may as well use question with the wolf/Why he hath made the ewe bleat for the lamb'** (IV.1.3–4)
2. Shylock on the theme of justice: **'If you deny me, fie upon your law:/There is no force in the decrees of Venice.'** (IV.1.101–2)
3. Portia on the theme of mercy: **'The quality of mercy is not strain'd,/It droppeth as the gentle rain from heaven'** (IV.1.182–3)
4. Bassanio on the theme of friendship: **'life itself, my wife, and all the world,/Are not with me esteem'd above thy life'** (IV.1.282–3)
5. Portia's abilities – Gratiano, mocking Shylock: **'an upright judge, a learned judge!'** (IV.1.321)

Note it!

Audiences in Shakespeare's day would have enjoyed Shylock's downfall, but we may find the 'mercy' offered to him ungenerous: he loses his lands and his religion, and his wealth passes to the daughter who betrayed him.

Exam focus

How can I write about Portia at the trial?

You can comment on how Portia's character is presented.

Portia demonstrates judgement, intelligence and wisdom. The poetic symbol of the 'quality of mercy' falling from heaven gives Shylock the chance to redeem himself. But in refusing her appeal he seals his own fate. Portia has placed herself on the side of law, reason and Christian charity, all elements designed to appeal to Shakespeare's audience at the time.	Topic sentence/overall point
	Quotation and literary term
	Explanation of point
	Further comment on audience effect

Now you try!

Finish this paragraph about Shylock's vengeful character. Use one of the quotations from the list.

Shylock is presented as absolutely set on revenge in this scene, as Antonio's comparison..

PLOT AND STRUCTURE Act V

Five key things about Act V

1. There is a **shift** in pace and tone as the action moves to **Belmont** and **night-time**.
2. The **final elements** of the **plot**, including the ring subplot, are **resolved**.
3. **Further news is revealed** regarding the **successful return** of some of **Antonio's ships**.
4. The mood **is enhanced by music**, and lyrical dialogue between **Jessica and Lorenzo**.
5. The themes of **love, friendship** and **appearance and reality** are revisited.

What happens at the start of Act V?

- Lorenzo and Jessica, who are waiting at Belmont, talk about classical lovers who were together on **'such a night'** as this one.
- Stephano brings news of Portia's return and Lancelot reports that Bassanio is also on his way to Belmont.
- Lorenzo requests music, although Jessica states she is **'never merry'** when she hears **'sweet music'**.

What happens next?

- Portia and Nerissa arrive first, and instruct the servants and Lorenzo and Jessica not to reveal to Bassanio and Gratiano that they have been absent.
- Bassanio, Gratiano and Antonio arrive. Portia pretends to be meeting Antonio for the first time. Gratiano and Nerissa argue over the ring given to the clerk (Nerissa) of the lawyer (Balthazar/Portia).
- Portia has fun reprimanding Gratiano for giving the ring away; Bassanio is forced to admit he has done the same.
- The trick is revealed as the ring that Portia then gives to Antonio to hand to Bassanio is the original.
- Portia presents a letter from her cousin Dr Bellario which explains her role of lawyer. She also reveals that three of Antonio's ships have safely returned.
- Nerissa breaks the final piece of news – that Lorenzo and Jessica will inherit all Shylock's possessions on his death.

Five key quotations

1. Lorenzo on the theme of love: 'In such a night/Did Jessica steal from a wealthy Jew/And with an unthrift love did run from Venice' (V.1.14–16)
2. Mood and setting – Lorenzo: 'How sweet the moonlight sleeps upon this bank!' (V.1.54)
3. Dramatic irony – Portia to Gratiano: 'You give your wife too unkind a cause of grief;/And 'twere to me, I should be mad at it.' (V.1.175–6)
4. Portia's humour: 'I'll have that doctor for my bedfellow.' (V.1.233)
5. Antonio on Portia's qualities: 'Sweet lady, you have given me life and living' (V.1.286)

Note it!

The final scene turns the play from what might have been tragedy to comedy. Note the elements of comedy: misunderstandings resolved, lovers reunited, wealth going to those who deserve it – although some audiences may question how deserving Jessica is.

Exam focus

How can I write about mood?

You can comment on how the mood of the scene is created.

The opening to the act could not be more different in mood and tone from the previous one. The beautiful	Topic sentence/overall point
night-time setting and the harmonious dialogue between Lorenzo and Jessica suggest peace and unity.	Develops point
The references to classical lovers who met on 'such a night' add depth to the lovers' feelings. And yet, the	Quotation supports point
examples given all end tragically. So perhaps this is an omen for Jessica and Lorenzo.	Interpretation raises questions

Now you try!

Finish this paragraph about how humour or dramatic irony is brought into the scene. Use one of the quotations from the list.

The humorous mood is created by Portia's joke to Bassanio, telling him ....

My progress   Needs more work ☐   Getting there ☐   Sorted! ☐   **17**

PLOT AND STRUCTURE Form and structure

Three key things about form and structure

1. The plot has a **classic five-part structure**: exposition, rising action, climax, falling action, resolution.
2. There are three **interweaving plot-lines**: the **revenge** plot; the **casket/love** plot; the **Jessica elopement** plot.
3. Although the play takes place over three months, there is a sense of **increasing pace and drama**.

Which is the most important plot in the play?

- The revenge plot is the most important: the court-room scene forms the dramatic climax, and the stakes are high: life and death!
- The narrative journeys of Antonio and Shylock mirror each other: both suffer a fall, but Antonio is rescued, whereas Shylock is destroyed.
- The revenge story powerfully engages the emotions, particularly through Shylock's speeches and Portia's plea for mercy.

What other structural elements are important?

- The movement between the real world of Venice and fantasy-like Belmont create changes in pace, mood and tone.
- The fairy-tale structure of the casket test with its riddles and pattern of three suitors is separate from, and yet intertwines with, the other plots.
- Act V, with its music, lyricism and humour, retrospectively changes the play from being almost a tragedy to conventional comedy.

How does time work in the play?

- Shakespeare cleverly makes the audience wait: we find out about the casket test and Morocco in Act I Scene 2, but it is not until Act II, after the bond is agreed, that Morocco arrives.
- The potential risk to Antonio's ships is rumoured early in the play, and there is then a drip-feed of news until the full extent of his losses (or so it seems) is confirmed in his letter of Act III Scene 3.

Five key quotations

1. Sarlarino foreshadows the loss of Antonio's ships: 'What harm a wind too great might do at sea.' (I.1.24)

2. The main revenge plot – Shylock: 'I will feed fat the ancient grudge I bear him' (I.3.42)

3. The play's fairy-tale element – Nerissa to Portia: 'will no doubt never be chosen by any rightly but one who you shall rightly love' (I.2.30–1)

4. The Jessica/Lorenzo subplot:
'O Lorenzo,/If thou keep promise, I shall end this strife,/Become a Christian and thy loving wife.' (II.3.18–20)

5. Dramatic climax – Portia: 'Why then, thus it is:/You must prepare your bosom for his knife.' (IV.1.242–3)

Note it!

The fairy-tale element of the casket test not only links to the themes of love and appearance/reality, but gives Belmont a different tone from that of Venice. It also lends structure, with the repeating pattern of the three suitor scenes.

Exam focus

How can I write about formal elements of the play? AO1 AO2

You can write about how Act IV uses the form of a trial to build a dramatic climax.

> Shakespeare uses the form of a trial, with evidence, a plaintiff (Shylock), an accused (Antonio) and a lawyer (Portia) to create dramatic tension. This is the climax of the plot as Portia tells Antonio to prepare your bosom for his knife.' This represents a high point for Shylock, but soon he is on a downward path.

Overall point about form

The elements of the form

Quotation links to dramatic structure

Links to character

Now you try!

Finish this paragraph about how different types of plot contribute to the play. Use one of the quotations from the list.

The Jessica/Lorenzo love subplot benefits the play in a number of ways: firstly by .....

1. Look at this ideas map representing Act I. Is there anything else you could add?

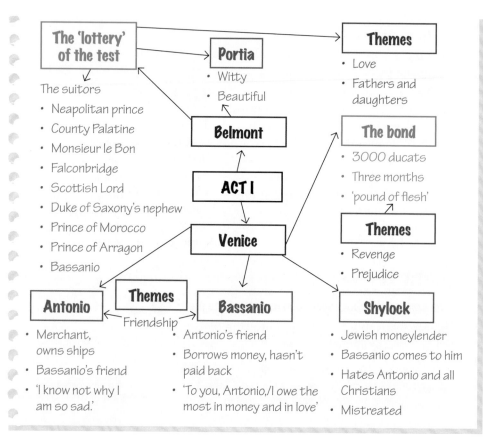

2. Create your own ideas map for one of the other acts in the play.

Quick quiz

Answer these quick questions about plot and structure.

1. In which city does the play begin?
2. What mood is Antonio in at the start of the play?
3. Why does Bassanio want to borrow money from Antonio?
4. Who devised the 'lottery' of the test for Portia?

5. What amount of money does Bassanio ask to borrow from Shylock?
6. Who decides to leave Shylock's employment?
7. What is Jessica going to take with her when she escapes from her father?
8. Which casket does Morocco choose?
9. What worrying news is reported about Antonio?
10. Who chooses the silver casket?
11. Who gives Shylock news of Jessica's reckless spending?
12. What does Portia give Bassanio as a symbol of their love?
13. How does Bassanio find out about Antonio's losses?
14. What does Portia tell Nerissa they are going to do after Bassanio has left?
15. Which important person in Venice fails to change Shylock's mind?
16. What name does Portia adopt as a lawyer?
17. What does the bond *not* allow Shylock to take?
18. What possible punishment does Shylock face but avoid?
19. What does Portia/Balthazar ask for in payment for her services?
20. What other good news does Antonio receive in the final scene?

Power paragraphs

Write a **paragraph** in response to **each of these questions**. For each, try to **use one quotation** you have learned.

1. In what ways do two of the main plots of the play link together in Act I?
2. How do Acts IV and V contrast in mood?

Exam practice

Re-read the section in Act I Scene 2 from line 21 'O me, the word "choose"!' to line 36 'level at my affection'.

Why is this moment significant in the text as a whole? Write **two paragraphs** explaining your ideas.

You could comment on:

● how the casket test is important to the play as a whole
● how Shakespeare explores any key themes or ideas.

Five key things about Jews and Christians in Shakespeare's day

1. Most families in England subscribed to **Christian values** of the time.
2. Most **children** in England were **baptised** into the **Church of England** soon after they were born.
3. Around the world, there had been a long **history of Jews** being **exiled** from or suppressed in many states, including England.
4. It is unlikely that **Shakespeare's audience** would have known **any Jews personally** as they had been **expelled from England 300 years earlier**.
5. **Playwrights** such as **Christopher Marlowe** also created **Jewish characters**.

How did Christian values affect English society?

- Children were taught the main aspects of Christian faith and Bible stories.
- Henry VIII had founded the Church of England in opposition to the Roman Catholic faith, but Elizabeth I allowed most people to practise other faiths privately.

How were Jews treated in Shakespeare's time?

- King Edward I had expelled the Jews from England in 1290. Prejudice had grown and they were viewed as heretics (people whose beliefs did not agree with the official beliefs of the Church).
- They were also blamed by many for catastrophes, such as the plague.
- In 1594, one of the Queen's doctors, a Portuguese Jew named Roderigo Lopez, was tried and executed for attempting to poison the Queen. Racial propaganda was a key factor in his trial.
- Christopher Marlowe's play *The Jew of Malta* features a Jew, named Barabas, who is presented much less sympathetically than Shylock.

Why is the issue of money-lending so important in the play?

- Ancient biblical tradition suggested it was immoral to lend money with interest, yet in 1571 Parliament legalised charging interest, provided it was beneath 10 per cent.
- In the absence of Jewish moneylenders in England, many English merchants lent money for interest.

Three key quotations

1. Bassanio on debt: 'my chief care/Is to come fairly off from the great debts/Wherein in my time, something too prodigal,/Hath left me gag'd.' (I.1.127–30)

2. Shylock on money-lending: **'Signior Antonio, many a time and oft/ In the Rialto you have rated me/About my monies and my usances.'** (I.3.101–3)

3. Treatment of Jews – Portia in court: **'The Jew shall have all justice; soft, no haste;/He shall have nothing but the penalty.'** (IV.1.319–20)

Note it!

Bassanio's situation, of being heavily in debt, was true of many of the prominent noblemen of Shakespeare's time, including the Earl of Essex, the Earl of Leicester and the Earl of Southampton.

Exam focus

How do I link context to the play?

You can talk about the different attitudes to Shylock as a Jew.

By the end of the play, it seems that Shylock has been reduced to the stereotypical Jew, the medieval villain who was foremost in audiences' minds. Portia tells the court, 'The Jew shall have all justice' while Gratiano wants him hanged but the duke pardons him. It seems that Shakespeare wishes the New Testament idea of Christian mercy to win over the Old Testament 'eye for an eye'.

Reference to context	
Relevant quotation	
Thoughtful analysis	
Point summarising opposing attitudes	

Now you try!

Finish this paragraph about ideas relating to the play's context. Use one of the quotations from the list.

The issue of lending or accumulating money is central to the play, as is shown when Shylock mentions ....

SETTING AND CONTEXT Settings

Five key things about the play's settings

1. **Contrast** in settings: **Venice** is a real place in **Northern Italy**; **Belmont** (meaning 'beautiful hill') is a **fictitious** one.
2. **Venice** in **Shakespeare's day** was probably the most **important trading centre** in the **world**.
3. The play suggests **Venice** is **bustling** and a **melting-pot** of people.
4. **Belmont's isolation** from Venice gives it an almost **fairy-tale quality**.
5. **Italy** was a **common setting** for many of **Shakespeare's comedies**.

What impression of Venice is given in the play?

- Numerous references to business, boats and overseas trade remind the audience of Venice's importance and its reputation: Tubal mentions Genoa, in Act III Scene 1, a rival for Venice's trade and influence.
- Tubal suggests Venice's diversity. While not mentioned in the play, after 1516, by law Jewish people in Venice had to return to a separate district (the ghetto) at night.
- The city's laws are overseen by the duke, but he, too, is subject to them.

What impression is given of Belmont?

- Belmont could be described as feminine – initially there are no men there (although Portia's father casts a shadow over her life).

- As the location of the casket test, with princes coming to try and win Portia, it reminds audiences of fairy-tale castles or mythical challenges.
- It is the setting for most of the play's humour – for example, Portia's witty summing-up of her suitors, the ring trick and its outcome.
- Belmont has a lyrical, musical quality, best expressed at the start of Act V as Jessica and Lorenzo talk together in the moonlight.

How is the Italianate setting important?

- Some of the comedy derives from the stock characters of **commedia dell'arte**, such as witty servants and wealthy, often foolish, older men.
- Italy was seen in Shakespeare's day as exotic, passionate and intriguing.

Three key quotations

1. Fairy-tale Belmont – Bassanio: 'the four winds blow in from every coast/Renowned suitors, and her sunny locks/Hang on her temples like a golden fleece' (I.1.168–70)

2. Venice as a place of trade – Antonio: 'Try what my credit can in Venice do' (I.1.180)

3. Venice as a melting-pot – Salarino: 'I reason'd with a Frenchman yesterday/Who told me, in the Narrow Seas that part/The French and English, there miscarried/A vessel' (II.8.28–31)

Note it!

The range of Portia's suitors, from many different countries, reminds the audience that the Venice region (of which Belmont is part) is an exotic centre of travel and fortune-seeking.

Exam focus

How can I write about how the setting contributes to the play's themes?

You can write about Venice's role in the play.

The image of Venice as a place of finance and fortune is made clear in the play. For example, Antonio's	Contextual overview point
reputation as a merchant is on the line when he tells Bassanio to 'Try what my credit can in Venice do'. The	Quotation and evidence
use of the term 'credit' means both Antonio's monetary status and his personal reputation. In this way, the	Language analysis
Rialto (Venice's business centre) is inextricably linked to Antonio's fate and, ultimately, his life.	Summary point

Now you try!

Write a paragraph about a different setting in the play. Use one of the quotations from the list above.

Shakespeare introduces the setting of Belmont through Bassanio's ....

SETTING AND CONTEXT Gender

Five key things about gender in the play

1. **Daughters** – Jessica and Portia – are presented as **being trapped** in different ways by their **fathers**.

2. **Portia** is also presented as an **independent** and **intelligent** young woman.

3. **Men's financial** and **legal power** is made clear: **Lorenzo** benefits from **Shylock's fall** and **Bassanio** gains **possession** of **Portia's fortune by marriage**.

4. **Friendship** and **conflict** between **men** forms the central focus of the **main plot**.

5. The play **ends** with the **traditional marrying-off** of **three couples**.

How is male power represented as the play develops?

- Men make the deal related to the bond and the loan arises from male friendship, which is presented in the play as being equal in strength to the relationship between any man and woman.

- Portia's dead father exerts control over her with his will, using the casket test to choose her husband.

- The court-room scene features a male plaintiff and accused, a male lawyer (albeit a woman disguised) and the duke, who passes ultimate sentence on Shylock.

In what ways is Portia empowered?

- Although disguised as a man, Portia's performance in the role of lawyer makes it clear that she is perfectly capable of succeeding in it.

- Shakespeare gives her the great set-piece speech of the play (about mercy) and shows her to be both witty and wise.

- However, her speech to Bassanio in Act III Scene 2 makes clear her duties and obligations to him.

How are other women presented?

- Nerissa is represented as a lively and willing companion to Portia and outwits Gratiano.
- Jessica is shown to be wilful in escaping her father, and does not behave as a dutiful daughter might be expected to behave.

Three key quotations

1. The issue of Portia's inheritance: 'the will of a living daughter curbed by the will of a dead father' (I.2.23–4)
2. Fathers and daughters – Shylock: 'My own flesh and blood to rebel!' (III.1.31)
3. Portia on marriage: 'her gentle spirit/Commits itself to yours to be directed/As from her lord, her governor, her king' (III.2.163–5)

Quick quiz

Answer these quick questions about setting and context.

1. What Christian ceremony was held for babies in England during Shakespeare's time?
2. When were Jews banned from England?
3. What was the name of the Jewish character in Christopher Marlowe's play?
4. Who was Roderigo Lopez?
5. What does 'Belmont' mean?
6. What was the business district in Venice called?
7. What other Italian city-state is mentioned in the play?
8. What does Bassanio gain from marrying Portia?
9. How does Portia's dead father continue to control her after he has died?
10. How does Portia prove she is as skilled in law as any man?

Power paragraphs

Choose one key setting or context related to the play. Write **two paragraphs** explaining how Shakespeare makes use of this setting or context in relation to either a) Portia's character or b) the theme of love and friendship. For each, try to use **one or more of the quotations** you have learned.

My progress   Needs more work ☐   Getting there ☐   Sorted! ☐   27

Five key things about Shylock

1. Shylock is a **Jewish moneylender** with a **daughter, Jessica**.
2. He is true to his **faith** but uses **biblical references** to justify his **business practices**.
3. He **seeks revenge** through the **bond** for the way he is **treated by Antonio** and **other Christians**.
4. He feels **doubly betrayed** as **Jessica** runs off with a **Christian** and **steals his money**.
5. He **pursues Antonio's death relentlessly** and refuses to accept any other form of repayment.

What do we learn about Shylock in Act I Scene 3?

- We first see Shylock negotiating the terms of the loan to Antonio with Bassanio.
- He is initially keen to be assured that Antonio can be relied on to repay his debt.
- He doesn't have ready money to lend, but states he will borrow it from another Jew, Tubal.
- He complains openly about how he and other Jews have been treated by Christians, but keeps the depth of his hatred hidden.
- Despite this, he is able to persuade Antonio to sign up to his **'merry sport'**.

How does Shylock's desire for revenge develop?

- Shylock is reported as being furious about Jessica's flight with a Christian and with his money. (Act II Scene 8)
- He argues forcefully that Jews are as human as Christians, and openly expresses his desire for revenge. (Act III Scene 1)
- In Act III Scene 2, it is reported that **'Twenty merchants'** and the **'duke himself'** failed to persuade him to relent, and that he will start legal action against the state if he does not get justice.
- In Act IV Scene 1, he relishes Antonio's imminent death.
- Once he realises he cannot take his **'pound of flesh'** he asks for financial repayment, but is finally left broken by the punishment he faces.

Five key quotations

1. Shylock's faith: **'I will not eat with you, drink with you, nor pray with you.'** (I.3.32–3)
2. Shylock's hate: **'If I can catch him once upon the hip,/I will feed fat the ancient grudge I bear him.'** (I.3.41–2)
3. Prejudice towards Shylock – Antonio: **'I am as like .../To spit on thee again, to spurn thee too.'** (I.3.125–6)
4. Shylock's eloquence: **'I am a Jew. Hath not a Jew eyes? Hath not a Jew hands, organs, dimensions, senses, affections, passions?'** (III.1.52–3)
5. Jessica's dislike of him: **'Our house is hell'** (II.3.2)

Note it!

One interesting parallel between Antonio and Shylock is that Shylock, too, has to borrow from someone – Tubal – to lend money to Antonio. It is never explained how Tubal would have got his money back if Antonio had died.

Exam focus

How can I write about Shylock at the start? (AO1)

You can comment on how Shylock is cunning at the beginning of the play.

At the start, it is possible Antonio misjudges Shylock's depth of hatred. Shylock reveals in an aside to the audience that he has an 'ancient grudge' against Antonio suggesting that the ill-feeling between them has existed for some time. Antonio seems to think that if it is a purely business transaction then it doesn't matter what they feel about each other. This makes him vulnerable to Shylock's clever proposal of a 'merry sport'.

- Topic sentence refers to Shylock at start
- Relevant quotation is fluently embedded
- Develops idea
- Links to new point about Shylock's cleverness

Now you try!

Finish this paragraph about how others feel about Shylock. Use one of the quotations from the list.

Shakespeare emphasises the dislike for Shylock when Antonio...

Five key things about Antonio

1. Antonio is the **wealthy** and **influential** merchant of the title, but is **not a typical** protagonist.
2. He has a **close friendship** with **Bassanio** which leads to him **misjudging Shylock**.
3. He seems to be **melancholy and reflective**.
4. He **does not hide his dislike for Shylock**, nor does he apologise for his past treatment of him.
5. He **respects the law**, whether it is against him or, as it is finally, on his side.

What do we learn about Antonio at the start of the play?

- In Act I Scene 1, we learn that he looks and feels sad but does not know why.
- He has many ships at sea, in many different places.
- He has lent Bassanio money before, and hasn't got it back, but is more than willing for his **'credit'** to raise further money to help his friend.
- In Act I Scene 3, we find out he lends money without interest, damaging Shylock's business.
- He trusts Shylock and agrees to the conditions of the bond; he is confident his own ventures will come back safely and repay the loan well in advance.

How does Antonio change as the play goes on?

- He disappears from the action during the middle of the play, though we hear reports of how his ships are doing.
- Others report Bassanio's departure and its effect on Antonio, his **'eye being big with tears'**. (Act II Scene 8)
- About to be jailed, Antonio urges respect for the law, saying that without it the reputation of Venice would be damaged. (Act III Scene 3)
- He seems to accept his death as inevitable and due to his own weakness. (Act IV Scene 1)
- Once he is saved, he demands that Shylock becomes a Christian and that all the Jew's possessions go to Lorenzo and Jessica on his death. (Act IV Scene 1)

Five key quotations

1. Antonio's state of mind: 'A stage where every man must play a part,/ And mine a sad one' (I.1.78–9)
2. Shylock on Antonio's treatment of Jews: 'He hates our sacred nation, and he rails/Even there where merchants do congregate/On me' (I.3.43–5)
3. Antonio's feelings for Bassanio – Solanio: 'I think he only loves the world for him.' (II.8.51)
4. Antonio's respect for the law: 'The duke cannot deny the course of law' (III.3.26)
5. His acceptance of his fate: 'I am a tainted wether of the flock,/ Meetest for death' (IV.1.114–15)

Note it!

Other than lend Bassanio money, Antonio does not *do* anything in the play, and could be seen as a passive figure, almost a loner, notwithstanding his reported treatment of Shylock.

Exam focus

How can I write about Antonio at the start of the play? AO1

You can comment on Antonio's low spirits.

> At the start of the play, Antonio is a bit of a mystery. He comments that the world is 'A stage where every man must play a part,/And mine a sad one', a metaphor implying that it is his role to be sad, though he does not say why. As the act progresses we might think it is because he is going to lose his best friend to marriage. However, he does nothing to prevent this; in fact, he goes out of his way to raise the money to make it happen.

Topic sentence sums up Antonio at this point

Quotation and language analysis

Suggests explanation

Develops contrasting evidence

Now you try!

Finish this paragraph about how Antonio responds to other characters or events. Use one of the quotations from the list.

Shakespeare presents Antonio's understanding of how Venice operates when he states...

Five key things about Bassanio

1. Bassanio is a **Venetian nobleman** and **close friend of Antonio**.
2. He **mistrusts Shylock** from the start, but **underestimates** his resolve.
3. He has **wasted money** and **not paid back debts**, but ultimately **succeeds** in gaining wealth.
4. He **loves Portia** and shows **good judgement** in choosing the **lead casket**.
5. His sense of **what is right** makes him give up his **ring** to Balthazar (Portia).

What do we learn about Bassanio at the start of the play?

- Bassanio has wasted both his own fortune and money given to him by Antonio. (Act I Scene 1)
- He is optimistic and persuasive, convincing Antonio to lend him money to woo Portia. (Act I Scene 1)
- He has misgivings about the bond with Shylock, but does not prevent Antonio agreeing to it. (Act I Scene 3)
- He is described by Nerissa as **'a scholar and a soldier'** and as **'best deserving'** Portia. (Act I Scene 2)

How does Bassanio develop as the play goes on?

- He warns Gratiano about excessive behaviour, suggesting he is starting to mature. (Act II Scene 2)
- He demonstrates wisdom in choosing the lead casket, recognising that value cannot be judged by outward appearance. (Act III Scene 2)
- He becomes wealthy as a result of winning Portia: gaining her house and servants, and Portia herself. (Act III Scene 2)
- He is forced to admit to Portia that is he poor and that he has borrowed money, which has endangered Antonio. (Act III Scene 2)
- He is moved by Antonio's letter requesting him to return to Venice, and later admits he would sacrifice anything to save Antonio. (Act IV Scene 1)
- He reluctantly gives up his ring, but confesses to Portia, showing honourable motives. (Act V Scene 1)

Five key quotations

1. Bassanio's spending: 'like a wilful youth/That which I owe is lost' (I.1.146–7)

2. Portia's compliment about him to Nerissa: 'I remember him well, and I remember him worthy of thy praise.' (I.2.109–10)

3. His mistrust of Shylock: 'I like not fair terms and a villain's mind.' (I.3.175)

4. His good judgement: 'So may the outward shows be least themselves:/ The world is still deceiv'd with ornament.' (III.2.73–4)

5. How he values friendship: 'Here is a letter, lady,/The paper as the body of my friend,/And every word in it a gaping wound' (III.2.261–3)

Note it!

Bassanio is angered by Shylock's refusal to take payment in Act IV Scene 1, calling him a **'cruel devil'**, but it is Gratiano who seems to revel in Shylock's downfall. Perhaps Bassanio is ashamed of his inability to persuade Shylock to relent, and of being the cause of his friend's death sentence.

Exam focus

How can I write about Bassanio at the start of the play? AO1

You can comment on Bassanio's closeness to Antonio in the opening scene.

It is clear how close Bassanio is to Antonio from the very first scene. Although Bassanio admits he has lost his fortune and money lent him by Antonio 'like a wilful youth', Antonio readily lends him more. The adjective 'wilful' suggests Bassanio recognises he is someone keen to get his own way. But this wilfulness, seen in his desire to win Portia, perhaps prevents him from fully understanding Shylock's plan.

Topic sentence defines Bassanio at this point

Quotation supports point

Analyses language

Develops point

Now you try!

Finish this paragraph about the close bond between Bassanio and Antonio. Use one of the quotations from the list.

Shakespeare shows that Bassanio feels deeply about ....

Five key things about Portia

1. Portia is a **Venetian noblewoman** who lives on an island called **Belmont**.
2. Her **future** depends on her **dead father's will** which includes a **riddling test** for any suitors.
3. She is **pleased** when the **Princes of Morocco** and **Arragon fail** the casket test, and **Bassanio** wins her instead.
4. She shows **wit**, **intelligence** and **judgement** in playing the part of the **lawyer, Balthazar**.
5. Her **speech** about the **'quality of mercy'** forms part of the **dramatic and emotional climax** of the play.

What do we learn about Portia at the start of the play?

- Portia feels constrained by the conditions of her dead father's will. (Act I Scene 2)
- She has a lively mind, as shown by her descriptions of her would-be suitors. (Act I Scene 2)
- She is courteous towards the Princes of Morocco and Arragon, but is happy when they fail the test. (Act II Scene 7 and Act II Scene 9)

- She worries that Bassanio **'choosing wrong'** will mean she loses him. (Act III Scene 2)
- When Bassanio chooses the correct casket, she gives him her ring, as a symbol of the passing of all that is hers into his possession. (Act III Scene 2)

How does Portia develop as the play goes on?

- On hearing of Antonio's debt, Portia's generosity is shown in her offer to pay the full amount several times over. (Act III Scene 2)
- She shows trust in releasing Bassanio to go and help Antonio. (Act III Scene 2)
- She demonstrates courage in entrusting Lorenzo and Jessica with her house and going disguised as a man to Venice. (Act III Scene 4)
- As Balthazar, she shows wisdom and eloquence in court. (Act IV Scene 1)
- She is presented as witty and independent in devising and revealing the ring plot. (Act IV Scene 2 and Act V Scene 1)

Five key quotations

1. Portia's enforced lack of independence: 'Is it not hard, Nerissa, that I cannot choose one, nor refuse none?' (I.2.24–5)

2. Her relief at Morocco failing the casket test: 'Let all of his complexion choose me so.' (II.7.79)

3. Portia on her value when accepting Bassanio: 'the full sum of me/Is sum of something: which to term in gross/Is an unlesson'd girl, unschool'd, unpractis'd' (III.2.157–9)

4. Her eloquence – describing mercy: 'mightiest in the mightiest, it becomes/The throned monarch better than his crown.' (IV.1.186–7)

5. Her wit: 'Now by mine honour which is yet mine own,/I'll have that doctor for my bedfellow.' (V.1.232–3)

Note it!

Many critics believe Portia to be one of Shakespeare's most rounded female characters, both in her characterisation and in her impact on the play's outcome. All three main male characters are affected by her actions: Antonio is saved, Shylock defeated and Bassanio helped – and out-witted!

Exam focus

How can I write about Portia at the start of the play? (AO1)

You can comment on Portia's feelings of being trapped.

Portia is presented as frustrated at how her father's will affects her choice of husband. She complains to Nerissa of being unable to 'choose one, nor refuse none'. All she can do is verbally dismiss unsuitable men in humorous ways. Later, however, this desire for independence is perhaps what leads her to adopt the role of a male lawyer, enabling her to make her own judgements.	Topic sentence defines Portia at this point
	Quotation supports point
	Develops explanation
	Links to her later behaviour

Now you try!

Finish this paragraph about how Portia behaves when she accepts Bassanio. Use one of the quotations from the list.

Shakespeare reveals that Portia, while showing independent thought, also thinks of herself as..

Three key things about Gratiano

1. Gratiano is **Bassanio's friend** and a **Venetian gentleman**.
2. He is initially presented as a **bit of a joker** who **loves talking**. Later, he agrees to act sensibly in order to accompany Bassanio to Belmont.
3. His **falls in love with Nerissa**, and is victim to the same ring trick as Bassanio.

What is his function in the play?

- Gratiano acts as a sort of clown-like figure – the alternative to Antonio's seriousness – and questions Antonio's melancholy behaviour in Act I Scene 1.
- In this role, he follows Bassanio to Belmont. He and Nerissa represent a more one-dimensional version of Bassanio and Portia's relationship.
- His hot-headed, angry responses to Shylock in Act IV Scene 1 contrasts with the measured, wise judgement of Portia.

Three key things about Nerissa

1. Nerissa is **Portia's maid** and her **confidante**.
2. She **advises Portia** on her suitors and **willingly helps her out** in the disguise plot.
3. She **falls in love with Gratiano**, and plays the same ring trick on him as Portia does on Bassanio.

What is her function in the play?

- Portia's character, plans and ideas are often revealed in her conversations with Nerissa.
- She acts as a rational voice who helps Portia accept the wisdom of her father's casket test.
- When playing a man's role, she is equally as adept as Portia.
- She contributes to the comic subplot of the rings in outwitting her husband.

Five key quotations

1. Bassanio on Gratiano's nonsense: 'Gratiano speaks an infinite deal of nothing' (l.1.114)

2. Gratiano's lack of manners: 'Thou art too wild, too rude, and bold of voice' (II.2.168)

3. Gratiano's anger towards Shylock: 'O be thou damn'd, inexecrable dog,/And for thy life let justice be accus'd!' (IV.1.128–9)

4. Nerissa's advice to Portia: 'Your father was ever virtuous; and holy men at their death have good inspirations.' (l.2.26–7)

5. Nerissa's wit, teasing Gratiano: 'that same scrubbed boy the doctor's clerk,/In lieu of this, last night did lie with me.' (V.1.261–2)

Note it!

Note how the parallel ring plot involving Nerissa and Gratiano is more comic, e.g. Gratiano tries to excuse himself saying Nerissa's was a **'paltry'** ring with some badly written verse on it, something it is unlikely Bassanio would have said about Portia's gift.

Exam focus

How can I write about Gratiano's character? AO1

You can comment on how Shakespeare uses Gratiano to heighten emotion.

One of Gratiano's functions in the court-room scene is to voice the emotions of the masses, who would like to see Shylock punished. His angry insult, telling Shylock he is a 'damn'd, inexecrable dog' contrasts with the measured, wise guidance from Portia. It demonstrates that he is unable to curb his hot-headed instincts. Whereas Bassanio seems to develop over the course of the play, Gratiano stands still.	Explains one of Gratiano's functions
	Well-chosen evidence
	Further explanation
	Summary contrasts his development with that of another character

Now you try!

Finish this paragraph about Nerissa's role. Use one of the quotations from the list.

One of Nerissa's core functions in the play is to act as a confidante ....

Three key things about Lorenzo

1. Lorenzo is one of a group of **Christian men** who are **friends with Bassanio**.
2. **Jessica**, Shylock's daughter, **is in love with Lorenzo** and they conspire together to escape her father.
3. He is **trusted** to look after **Portia's household** in Belmont while she is away.

What is his function in the play?

- Lorenzo and Jessica represent a bridge between the Christian and Jewish worlds in the play, albeit a bridge that is not entirely solid.
- Their relationship offers a third example of marriage which the audience can judge alongside those of Bassanio/Portia and Gratiano/Nerissa.
- His language in the final scene is witty, *lyrical* and reflective, contributing to a significant change in *mood* and *tone* from the high drama of Act IV to the harmony of Act V.

Three key things about Jessica

1. Jessica is **Shylock's daughter**; it is implied that her mother has died.
2. She **plots to flee from her father's house**, saying how unhappy she is, and when she marries Lorenzo, **converts to Christianity**.
3. She **escapes,** and is then reported as spending her father's money recklessly, increasing **his desire for revenge**.

What is her function in the play?

- Jessica contributes to the exploration of father/child relationships alongside those of Portia/Portia's late father and Lancelot/Old Gobbo.
- She exposes Shylock's cruelty, but could be viewed as vengeful herself.
- Although she becomes a Christian, Jessica is largely ignored by the other characters during the scenes in Belmont, which may suggest they do not entirely accept her.

Five key quotations

1. Lorenzo's commitment: 'Tell gentle Jessica/I will not fail her' (II.4.19–20)
2. Lorenzo's lack of money: 'In such a night/Did Jessica steal from a wealthy Jew/And with an unthrift love did run from Venice' (V.1.14–16)
3. Jessica's shame: 'Alack, what heinous sin is it in me/To be asham'd to be my father's child!' (II.3.15–16)
4. Tubal on her carefree spending: 'One of them showed me a ring that he had of your daughter for a monkey.' (III.1.105–6)
5. Jessica on religious faith to Lancelot: 'I shall be saved by my husband; he hath made me a Christian.' (III.5.16–17)

Note it!

Whether Lorenzo and Jessica's relationship is viewed sympathetically is open to interpretation. Their tender but mocking exchange at the start of Act V Scene 1 suggests mutual affection but the reality of marriage might prove different.

Exam focus

How can I write about Jessica's character? AO1

You can comment on how Shakespeare presents Jessica as contributing to Shylock's anger.

Shylock would probably have pursued Antonio regardless of circumstances, but Jessica's elopement pours fuel on the flames. When he finds out that the ring given him by his wife has been sold 'for a monkey' the audience may feel a little uneasy about Jessica's behaviour. The fact that she elopes with a Christian further adds to his list of grievances. While she is not the cause of his hatred, she contributes to it.

Explains one of Jessica's functions

Well-chosen evidence

Develops point

Summary point

Now you try!

Finish this paragraph about Lorenzo's contribution to the play. Use one of the quotations from the list.

In Act V Scene 1, when Lorenzo refers to himself as ....

Three key things about the Prince of Morocco

1. The Prince of Morocco is the **first of the three suitors** to take the casket test and **wrongly chooses the gold casket**.
2. He **boasts** of his military conquests but **behaves honourably** when he fails.
3. His **race and colour** are the cause of **discrimination** against him.

What is his function in the play?

- Morocco seems exotic, having come from so far away, and his praise of Portia establishes her worth.
- His appearance across two scenes (Act II Scene 1 and Act II Scene 7) draws out the dramatic tension between his arrival and making his choice.
- His choice of the gold casket develops the theme of appearance and reality.

Three key things about the Prince of Arragon

1. The Prince of Arragon is the **second of the three suitors** to take the casket test and **wrongly chooses the silver casket**.
2. While he doesn't fall into the trap of choosing the gold casket, his **vanity** makes him believe he should get **'as much as he deserves'**.
3. He **overstates his abilities**, and is rewarded with **'a fool's head'** in the silver casket.

What is his function in the play?

- Arragon was a kingdom of Spain, which was often at war with England. So portraying Arragon as foolish would have been popular with audiences.
- The fact that he rejects gold adds to the dramatic tension as the audience wonders if he will choose correctly and win Portia.
- The scene in which he chooses (Act II Scene 9) also adds to the tension of the main plot, coming immediately after the first hints that Antonio's ships may have **'miscarried'**.

Five key quotations

1. Morocco to Portia on his race: 'Mislike me not for my complexion' (II.1.1)
2. As an exotic visitor: 'the vasty wilds/Of wide Arabia are as thoroughfares now/For princes to come view fair Portia.' (II.7.41–3)
3. Morocco's misjudgement: 'Never so rich a gem/Was set in worse than gold.' (II.7.54–5)
4. Arragon's snobbery: 'I will not choose what many men desire,/Because I will not jump with common spirits' (II.9.30–1)
5. Arragon's foolishness: 'With one fool's head I came to woo,/But I go away with two.' (II.9.74–5)

Note it!

After the long, drawn-out wait between Morocco's first appearance and his choosing (Act II Scene 7), the appearances of Arragon (Act II Scene 9) and then Bassanio (Act III Scene 2) follow relatively quickly, adding to the sense of the plot speeding up towards its dramatic conclusion.

Exam focus

How can I write about Arragon's character? AO1

You can comment on how Shakespeare presents Arragon as foolish.

While Arragon avoids the trap of the gold casket, his vanity deceives him into choosing the silver casket. He refuses to choose 'what many men desire' (gold) because he doesn't want to be associated with 'common' people. Even his name sounds like a play on 'arrogant'. Bassanio may have faults, but he at least acknowledges them and does not boast of his great qualities.

- Main point about Arragon's character
- Well-chosen evidence
- Develops point with language detail
- Makes contrasting link to another character

Now you try!

Finish this paragraph about the role of Morocco. Use one of the quotations from the list.

Morocco has several functions, one of which is to bring a different world into the play through reference to places such as ....

1. Look at this ideas map about Shylock. Is there anything else you could add?

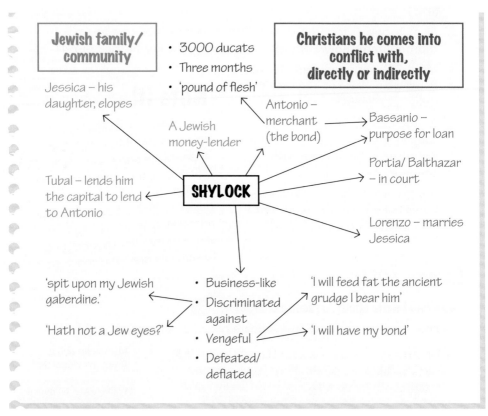

| Jewish family/ community | • 3000 ducats | Christians he comes into conflict with, directly or indirectly |

Jessica – his daughter, elopes

A Jewish money-lender

Tubal – lends him the capital to lend to Antonio

SHYLOCK

Antonio – merchant (the bond)

Bassanio – purpose for loan

Portia/ Balthazar – in court

Lorenzo – marries Jessica

'spit upon my Jewish gaberdine.'

'Hath not a Jew eyes?'

• Business-like
• Discriminated against
• Vengeful
• Defeated/ deflated

'I will feed fat the ancient grudge I bear him'

'I will have my bond'

2. Create your own ideas map for one of the other characters.

Quick quiz

Answer these quick questions about characters.

1. Who is Antonio's closest friend?
2. Who 'speaks an infinite deal of nothing'?
3. How does Nerissa describe Bassanio?
4. In what two ways does Portia show she is witty?
5. How has Antonio annoyed Shylock, in terms of business?
6. What sorts of abuse has Shylock suffered from Antonio?

7. Why is Shylock initially reluctant to lend money to Antonio?

8. Who does Shylock himself have to borrow money from?

9. Why does Bassanio have misgivings about the bond/loan?

10. What does Arragon's choice of casket tell us about him?

11. Who is Portia describing when she says 'Let all of his complexion choose me so'?

12. Why will Arragon leave with two fools' heads?

13. What does Jessica's purchase of a monkey imply?

14. What does the message found in the gold casket reveal about Morocco?

15. What does Portia do as she leaves Belmont that shows she trusts others?

16. What does Portia give to Bassanio to represent her sharing of her wealth and life with him?

17. How will Jessica's faith change when she marries Lorenzo?

18. How does Gratiano speak to Shylock in the courtroom scene?

19. What creature does Antonio compare himself to when saying how weak he is?

20. How does Nerissa's role in the play mirror Portia's?

Power paragraphs

Write **a paragraph** in response to **each of these questions**. For each, try to **use one quotation** you have learned from this section.

1. What impression do you get of Antonio once he realises that he is likely to die?

2. What function does Nerissa have in the play?

Exam practice

Re-read the section in Act II Scene 2 from Bassanio (line 172): 'Pray thee take pain/To allay with some cold drops of modesty' to Gratiano (line 187): 'you shall not gauge me/By what we do tonight.'

What do we learn about Gratiano from this conversation? Write **two paragraphs** explaining your ideas. You could comment on:

- Bassanio's concerns about him
- how Gratiano responds to those concerns.

My progress   Needs more work ☐   Getting there ☐   Sorted! ☐

THEMES Prejudice

Five key things about the theme of prejudice

1. The **anti-semitism** Shylock suffers is a **key motive** in driving the play's revenge plot.
2. **Shylock's response** to Christian mistreatment is itself a **form of prejudice**.
3. Crude **racial** stereotypes are seen elsewhere in the play, for example in Portia's suitors.
4. While racial stereotyping in the play may be intended as a **source of humour**, **modern audiences** immediately question such representations.
5. Prejudice **links to other key** themes such as appearance and reality.

How are ideas about anti-Semitism reflected in the main plot?

- Shylock makes Antonio's mistreatment of him explicit right at the start of the play by reporting how he has spat on his **'Jewish gaberdine'**.
- Jessica's desire to elope with a Christian lover endorses the idea that Shylock's mean nature extends even to his own flesh and blood.
- Stereotypes of Shakespeare's time about Jewish behaviour – greed, refusal to mix with Christian society, sharp business practices – are all embodied in Shylock.

How is prejudice shown in the casket subplot?

- Portia's light-hearted accounts of her suitors are based on national stereotypes (such as the Duke of Saxony's nephew's drinking and the English lord's inability to speak foreign languages).
- The Prince of Morocco urges Portia not to judge him by his skin colour, but then proves himself guilty of judging things on their appearance by selecting the gold casket.
- Arragon appears not to make the same error as Morocco, but vanity, a form of self-favouring prejudice – believing he deserves more than **'common spirits'**, instead leads him to choose wrongly.

Five key quotations

1. Shylock on anti-semitism: 'suff'rance is the badge of all our tribe' (I.3.105)

2. Shylock's own prejudice: 'I hate him for he is a Christian' (I.3.37)

3. Jewish stereotyping in Solanio's report of Shylock's loss of Jessica: '**Find the girl!/She hath the stones upon her and the ducats!**' (2.8.21–2)

4. Comic national stereotypes – Portia about Falconbridge: '**he hath neither Latin, French, nor Italian**' (I.2.64–5)

5. Race and appearance – Portia about Morocco: '**Let all of his complexion choose me so**' (II.7.79)

Note it!

One of the most intriguing things about the play is that we really don't know how Shakespeare wanted audiences to view Shylock. On the one hand, Shylock embodies all the anti-semitic stereotypes of the time, but conversely Shakespeare gives him some of the most poetic and moving speeches in the play.

Exam focus

How does Shakespeare explore ideas about prejudice? AO1

You can explore Antonio's prejudice towards Shylock.

Antonio is not presented in a particularly sympathetic way at the start of the play. When accused of spitting on Shylock's coat, he tells him he is 'as like …/To spit on thee again'. He does not try to flatter Shylock or apologise for his behaviour. The fact that Shylock says 'suff'rance is the badge of all our tribe' also tells the audience that Jews have had to get used to this mistreatment, but raises the question of why they should.	Introduces general idea
	Provides supporting quotation
	Develops explanation
	Offers deeper interpretation

Now you try!

Finish this paragraph about prejudice. Use one of the quotations from the list.

References in the play to Shylock's behaviour that confirm anti-semitic stereotypes include Solanio's ....

Five key things about the theme of money and commerce

1. Shylock's **loan to Antonio** and the **terms of its repayment** are at the heart of the **main plot** of the play.
2. **Antonio's fortunes** depend on the **success or failure** of his **ships** carrying cargo **abroad**.
3. The setting of Venice is significant as it was the world's **trading centre** at the time.
4. The motifs of **money**, **value** and **worth** run through the subplots of the casket test and Jessica's elopement.
5. **People are** treated like things to be traded: for example, **Bassanio gains wealth** in winning Portia, and Shylock treats Antonio's body as repayment.

How are ideas about money and trade reflected in the main plot?

- It is clear Antonio and Shylock have previously come into conflict about money. Shylock objects to the Christian practice of lending without interest which damages his business.
- Money and trade are linked to risk. There is no certainty that Bassanio will win Portia or that Antonio's ships will return.
- Money is directly linked to personal happiness and identity: Shylock is as outraged that his daughter stole from him as by her marrying a Christian.
- Shylock's wealth does not save him from Christian prejudice.

How are ideas about money developed through fathers/daughters?

- The casket test set by Portia's father is about value. The choice is between precious metals (gold, silver) and a more useful one (lead). Ironically Bassanio, in choosing the least precious, acquires Portia's lands and wealth.
- Money is linked to inheritance and marriage – wealth passing from father to daughter (Portia) but then ultimately into Bassanio's hands.
- In the court-room scene, this is mirrored in Shylock's wealth passing to Jessica and Lorenzo on Shylock's death.

Five key quotations

1. Attitudes to money – Shylock about Antonio: 'He was wont to lend money for a Christian courtesy; let him look to his bond.' (III.1.43–4)

2. Bassanio on the risk in trade: 'What, not one hit?/... not one vessel 'scape the dreadful touch/Of merchant-marring rocks?' (III.2.265–9)

3. Venice as a place of trade – Shylock about Antonio: 'I understand moreover upon the Rialto he hath a third at Mexico, a fourth for England, and other ventures' (I.3.16–18)

4. Shylock's anger: 'O my daughter!/ Fled with a Christian! O my Christian ducats!' (II.8.15–16)

5. Portia uses the language of money: 'The full sum of me/Is sum of something: which to term in gross/Is an unlesson'd girl, unschool'd, unpractis'd' (III.2.157–9)

Note it!

Motifs of value, for example, rings, run through the play. Shylock's **'turquoise'** ring is stolen by Jessica and used to purchase a mere monkey. Gratiano makes the mistake of saying Nerissa's ring is **'paltry'**. Only Bassanio recognises the true value of his ring, even if he does give it away.

Exam focus

How can I write about ideas linked to money? (AO1) (AO3)

You can comment on how Shakespeare relates money to identity.

Shakespeare explores how money is linked to identity.	General idea explored
It is hard to distinguish what hurts Shylock more – his daughter eloping with a Christian or her theft of his money. His cry, 'O my Christian ducats!' conflates the two and both are important factors in his hate for Antonio. This is proved later, when he refuses to take triple the loan repayment and instead pursues Antonio's death.	Development of idea
	Apt quotation and explanation
	Link to later action

Now you try!

Finish this paragraph about trade. Use one of the quotations from the list.

Shakespeare shows that trade and commerce are bound up with risk, notably when Bassanio...

THEMES Love and friendship

Five key things about the theme of love and friendship

1. **Friendships** range from that of **Antonio and Bassanio** at the play's heart, to those between **Portia/Nerissa**, **Bassanio/Gratiano** and **Jessica/Lancelot**.

2. The particularly **deep friendship** between **Antonio and Bassanio** is what leads Antonio to take **a dangerous risk**.

3. **Love** leads **characters** to undertake other potentially **life-changing decisions**: **Bassanio** to risk his future (and Antonio's life) to win Portia; **Jessica** to flee her father's house to be with Lorenzo.

4. **Self-love** is shown as **damaging** in the portrayal of the **Princes of Morocco** and **Arragon**.

5. The **union of the lovers in marriage** or with futures secure **traditionally ends Shakespearean comedy**.

How important is Antonio and Bassanio's friendship to the play?

- Their friendship could be said to border on love: various characters remark during the play on the strength of the bond between them.

- Although Antonio has money and has lent to Bassanio previously, without being repaid, he willingly lends to him again.

- Bassanio's strong friendship with Antonio is what drives him to immediately leave Portia and Belmont in order to try to save him.

- Bassanio's friendship with Gratiano could be seen as weaker largely because of Bassanio's greater status and nobility.

How are the different lovers meant to be viewed in the play?

- Bassanio's thoughtful judgement when he faces the casket test indicates that he is a good match for Portia.

- Jessica gives up her family and faith for Lorenzo, but her theft of jewels and money does not initially bode well for their future.

- When Jessica and Lorenzo speak at the start of Act V Scene 1, they compare themselves to tragic lovers from classical times, but they do seem well-matched in temperament.

Five key quotations

1. Antonio's help for Bassanio: 'be assur'd/My purse, my person, my extremest means/Lie all unlock'd to your occasions.' (I.1.137–9)

2. Bassanio's love or friendship for Antonio: 'I would lose all, ay, sacrifice them all/Here to this devil, to deliver you.' (IV.1.284–5)

3. Jessica on the dangers of love: 'Give him [Lorenzo] this letter, do it secretly./And so farewell: I would not have my father/See me in talk with thee.' (II.3.7–9)

4. Morocco's self-love: 'I do in birth deserve her [Portia], and in fortunes,/In graces, and in qualities of breeding' (II.7.32–3)

5. How comedies end – Gratiano: 'Well, while I live I'll fear no other thing/So sore as keeping safe Nerissa's ring.' (V.1.306–7)

Note it!

Note that Shakespeare blurs the boundary between love and friendship when it comes to Antonio and Bassanio's relationship. Clearly, the sort of friendship they have is more profound than that between Bassanio and Gratiano, or even Portia and Nerissa.

Exam focus

How can I write about love and friendship?

You could write about how Shakespeare shows love and friendship lead to danger.

Shakespeare explores how love and friendship lead people into danger. Jessica goes to extremes – telling Lancelot to 'secretly' take a letter to her lover, and dressing as a boy to disguise herself during the masque. She escapes with Lorenzo to Belmont, where they discover they are to inherit her father's wealth on his death. In this way, their gamble leads to a lucky outcome.	General idea explored
	Provides evidence
	Good knowledge of rest of play
	Links **themes** of danger and chance

Now you try!

Finish this paragraph about friendship. Use one of the quotations from the list.

Shakespeare shows that male friendship can be powerful as Bassanio's declaration

....

Five key things about the theme of revenge and justice

1. **Shylock's** pursuit of **revenge** forms the **central action** of the play.
2. **Revenge** is **linked** in the play to **mercy and forgiveness**, its **opposites**.
3. Revenge is both **personal** (Antonio's treatment of Shylock) and **general** (the treatment of Jews by Christians).
4. The question of **what justice is** runs through the play and **peaks in the trial**.
5. **Portia's role** as **lawyer** opens up **debates about gender** and enriches her characterisation.

How are ideas about revenge explored in the play?

- Shylock's revenge is introduced in Act I Scene 3 – but the implications of the bond only become clear as the play progresses.
- His desire for revenge is heightened by Jessica's elopement; when he can't find her, his anger towards Antonio is doubled.
- Antonio forgives Bassanio for putting him in danger. Portia and Nerissa both forgive their husbands for relinquishing the rings.
- Ultimately, revenge is self-destructive. Shylock leaves the stage a broken man.
- Revenge and forgiveness are linked to the Old and New Testament ideas of 'an eye for an eye' and, conversely, 'turning the other cheek'.

How does justice relate to characters and actions?

- Most modern audiences would feel that the reported treatment of Shylock by Antonio was unjust.
- Shylock believes strongly in Venetian justice, and uses his claim to it as a threat to the authority of the duke.
- The justice Shylock receives shows that the state upholds the rights of some citizens over those of others.
- Ironically, it is Portia (disguised as Balthazar) who dispenses justice in Act IV Scene 1. Women were not allowed to practise as lawyers in Shakespeare's time.

Five key quotations

1. Shylock's revenge plot: 'If I can catch him once upon the hip,/I will feed fat the ancient grudge I bear him.' (I.3.41–2)

2. Antonio's forgiveness: 'Give me your hand, Bassanio. Fare you well./ Grieve not that I am fall'n to this for you.' (IV.1.163–4)

3. Shylock's reasons: 'If you poison us, do we not die? And if you wrong us, shall we not revenge?' (III.1.58–9)

4. Portia's comment on The Lord's prayer (Christian): it 'doth teach us all to render/The deeds of mercy' (IV.1.199–200)

5. Bassanio on Portia's skills as lawyer: 'Most worthy gentleman, I and my friend/Have by your wisdom been this day acquitted/Of grievous penalties' (IV.1.406–8)

Note it!

As an important trading centre, Venice would need to be seen as a place of legal competence. This is why the duke cannot override the conditions of the bond. Shylock reminds him of this and Antonio says in Act III Scene 3 **'The duke cannot deny the course of law'**.

Exam focus

How can I write about revenge and forgiveness? AO1

You can show how Shakespeare contrasts these ideas in the court scene.

Through Portia, Shakespeare questions the validity of Shylock's idea of justice in the trial scene. She reminds him of the Christian Lord's prayer which 'doth teach us all to render/The deeds of mercy'. In other words, forgive those who have wronged us. When Shylock reacts against God's teachings, replying, 'My deeds upon my head!' – that he will take responsibility for his actions – Shakespeare turns the audience against him.	Overall point
	Apt quotation
	Supporting explanation
	Further quotation and development of point

Now you try!

Finish this further paragraph about revenge. Use one of the quotations from the list.

Shakespeare shows that Shylock is already thinking about revenge earlier in the play as ....

Five key things about the theme of appearance and reality

1. The idea of **not judging things by outward appearance** is a motif throughout the play, e.g. in the riddles of the casket test.

2. A number of characters **disguise themselves** for **serious purposes: Jessica** to **escape** from her father; **Portia** to **pretend to be a lawyer**.

3. Some characters **pretend** to be someone else for **comic effect: Lancelot** with **his father**; **Portia** and **Nerissa** as wives upset about **lost rings**.

4. A central **dramatic device** – the **bond** – is itself **a trap**.

5. **False information** heightens **tension**, e.g. reports of Antonio's ships all failing.

How is appearance and reality used in the first part of the play?

- Although Shylock reveals his desire for revenge in an aside, his offer to become friends fools Antonio into accepting the bond.

- Lancelot's tricking of his blind father into believing him dead mirrors Jessica's deception of her father – albeit for different purposes.

- The **'gossip'** in Venice suggests Antonio has lost a ship – building the audience's anxiety.

- The extent of Jessica's deceit of her father is revealed in her pre-planned escape and the way she spends his money.

How is appearance and reality developed in the second part of the play?

- Bassanio's choice of the lead casket indicates his potential as a good husband.

- Antonio's letter to Bassanio states **'my ships have all miscarried'**, leading the audience to believe he is doomed.

- Shylock appears to have won his case, but Portia reveals a loophole that saves Antonio, and destroys Shylock.

- The rings trick creates comedy as Portia and Nerissa shame their husbands about their unfaithful behaviour.

Five key quotations

1. Antonio believes Shylock's deceit: **'I'll seal to such a bond,/And say there is much kindness in the Jew.'** (I.3.148–9)

2. Jessica's physical disguise: **'Cupid himself would blush/To see me thus transformed to a boy.'** (II.6.39–40)

3. Bassanio foreshadows deceit in the trial scene: **'In law, what plea so tainted and corrupt/But, being season'd with a gracious voice,/Obscures the show of evil?'** (III.2.75–7)

4. False information questioned by Bassanio: **'But is it true, Salerio? Hath all his ventures failed? What, not one hit?'** (III.2.264–5)

5. Portia's humorous deceit: **'I'll not deny him anything I have,/No, not my body, nor my husband's bed'** (V.1.227–8)

Note it!

Self-deception is also an important factor in the play. The Princes of Morocco and Arragon are unable to see past their own vanity; Shylock allows himself to believe a Christian judge will uphold his rights.

Exam focus

How does Shakespeare use appearance and reality for dramatic effect? (AO1)

You can write about how Shakespeare uses dramatic irony to build tension.

Shakespeare creates dramatic tension in the bond scene. When Antonio agrees to 'seal to such a bond' and remarks on 'much kindness' in Shylock, the audience has already heard Shylock's aside about his plans to take revenge. This creates suspense: how will this deceit play out? Even in the trial scene, the duke believes that Shylock will pull out at the last minute – he is also deceived.	Dramatic effect introduced
	Explains how it works
	What the effect is
	Link to later action

Now you try!

Finish this paragraph about the theme elsewhere in the play. Use one of the quotations from the list.

Shakespeare shows how false information can mask the truth when Bassanio questions ....

THEMES Fathers and children

Five key things about the theme of fathers and children

1. Three father/child relationships are presented: Portia's **late father/Portia, Old Gobbo/Lancelot** and **Shylock/Jessica**.
2. The relationships range from **positive to negative**.
3. Ideas related to **patriarchy** (male-dominated society) **and power** are explored **through the relationships**.
4. **Daughters** are presented as **escaping their fathers** only to be **re-captured** (if willingly) **in marriage**.
5. The **separation of Portia from her father** works as a **dramatic device** to engage the audience's interest in her.

How are father/child relationships presented?

- Portia's father is absent from the play but his casket test influences the overall plot, and benefits Portia's life and that of Bassanio.

- Lancelot and his blind father, Old Gobbo, encounter each other in Act II Scene 2 in a comic scene with serious undertones. Lancelot, perhaps rather cruelly, pretends to be someone else, and says he (Lancelot) is dead.
- Shylock and Jessica appear together just once in Act II Scene 5. By then we know she plans to elope with Lorenzo. Later, we hear and witness Shylock's reaction to her escape.

What do we learn about the different relationships?

- Although Portia is initially frustrated by her father's will, Nerissa persuades her that he had her best interests at heart.
- Lancelot and his father do not initially appear to have a close relationship – Old Gobbo doesn't recognise his son – but he appears truly upset when led to believe Lancelot is dead. This prompts Lancelot to end the pretence.
- Shylock's controlling nature is evident in Act II Scene 5 when he instructs Jessica to keep away from the frivolity of the Christian masques. His later anger suggests he is utterly surprised by his daughter's betrayal.

Five key quotations

1. Nerissa on Portia's father: 'Your father was ever virtuous; and holy men at their death have good inspirations.' (I.2.26–7)

2. Lancelot on parent/child relationships: 'it is a wise father that knows his own child.' (II.2.71–2)

3. Portia on patriarchy: 'I was the lord/Of this fair mansion, master of my servants,/Queen o'er myself' (III.2.167–9)

4. Jessica's escape from Shylock: 'though I am a daughter to his blood/I am not to his manners.' (II.3.17–18)

5. Shylock's anger: 'I would my daughter were dead at my foot, and the jewels in her ear' (III.1.79–80)

Note it!

Coping without a father figure, or finding an alternative is a key trope of Shakespearean drama. For example, Prince Hamlet's father has recently died at the start of *Hamlet*, and Ferdinand loses his father in a storm in *The Tempest*. Here, Portia shows independence but relies on Nerissa's support.

Exam focus

How can I write about dutiful behaviour?

You can write about how Shakespeare explores the duty of children to parents.

Shakespeare suggests that duty is something a parent earns. While Jessica's rejection of her father may initially seem harsh, she claims she is not a daughter 'to his manners' and home life is 'hell'. There is a strong suggestion his joyless control is what drives her away. She recognises it is a 'crime' but seems to suffer no guilt after her escape, spending his money freely.	Key point
	Useful quotations develop point
	Further explanation
	Link to later action

Now you try!

Finish this paragraph about parents and children. Use one of the quotations from the list.

Shakespeare shows that Portia's father knew his child better than ....

My progress   Needs more work ☐   Getting there ☐   Sorted! ☐   55

1. Look at this ideas map representing the **theme** of revenge and justice. Is there anything else you could add?

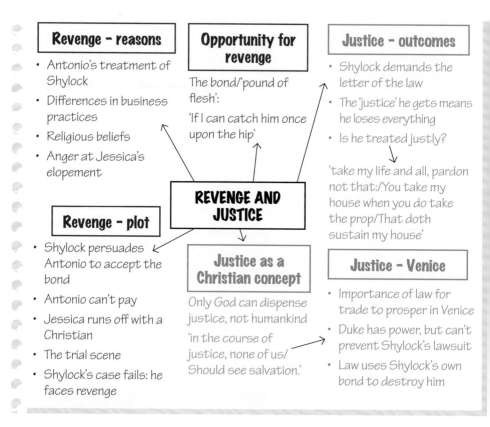

Revenge – reasons

- Antonio's treatment of Shylock
- Differences in business practices
- Religious beliefs
- Anger at Jessica's elopement

Opportunity for revenge

The bond/'pound of flesh':

'If I can catch him once upon the hip'

Justice – outcomes

- Shylock demands the letter of the law
- The 'justice' he gets means he loses everything
- Is he treated justly?

'take my life and all, pardon not that:/You take my house when you do take the prop/That doth sustain my house'

Revenge – plot

- Shylock persuades Antonio to accept the bond
- Antonio can't pay
- Jessica runs off with a Christian
- The trial scene
- Shylock's case fails: he faces revenge

REVENGE AND JUSTICE

Justice as a Christian concept

Only God can dispense justice, not humankind

'in the course of justice, none of us/ Should see salvation.'

Justice – Venice

- Importance of law for trade to prosper in Venice
- Duke has power, but can't prevent Shylock's lawsuit
- Law uses Shylock's own bond to destroy him

2. Create your own ideas map for one of the other themes.

Quick quiz

Answer these quick questions about themes.

1. How does the setting of Venice link to the theme of money and trade?
2. Why does Shylock object to Antonio's moneylending?
3. Shylock says he has heard Antonio has 'a third at Mexico, a fourth for England'. What is he referring to?
4. Why is it ironic that Bassanio chooses the cheapest, lead casket?

5. Name at least three pairs of friends in the play.
6. What sort of love is portrayed by Morocco and Arragon?
7. What does Jessica give up for Lorenzo?
8. Who says he would 'sacrifice … all' to save his friend from Shylock?
9. What ideas could be seen as opposite to 'revenge'?
10. Why does Shylock hold a personal grudge against Antonio?
11. What event heightens Shylock's desire for revenge?
12. How is Shylock's revenge turned against him in the trial scene by Portia?
13. What is ironic about Portia being the person to dispense justice?
14. What does Shylock say is his natural response if he is wronged?
15. Which three women disguise themselves as boys/men during the play?
16. Why is the casket test a good example of the saying, 'You shouldn't judge things by their appearance'?
17. How do Antonio's missing ships illustrate the theme of appearance and reality?
18. How does Portia's dead father continue to control her after his death?
19. What rather upsetting lie does Lancelot tell his blind father?
20. What sort of father does Lancelot say 'knows his own child'?

Power paragraphs

Write a **paragraph** in response to **each of these questions**. For each, try to **use one quotation** you have learned from this section.

1. What does Bassanio gain from marrying Portia?
2. In what ways does Shakespeare show the lack of understanding between fathers and their daughters?

Exam practice

Re-read the section from near the start of Act IV Scene I when Shylock speaks about his case to the duke (lines 35–62).

How does Shakespeare explore the idea of Shylock's justice in this speech? Write **two paragraphs** explaining your ideas. You could comment on:

- the threats Shylock makes to the duke
- why he is pursuing justice so relentlessly.

LANGUAGE Imagery and symbolism

Five key things about Shakespeare's imagery and symbolism

1. Shakespeare uses **powerful** images to convey **key** themes or ideas such as **prejudice, forgiveness** and **justice**.

2. He uses similes **and** metaphors to help the reader understand **characters and relationships**.

3. Settings and **relationships** in the play are symbolic **of wider concerns** such as Christian and Jewish conflict.

4. **Symbolism** enriches **language** and connects with **other texts and ideas**.

5. **Religious** allusions and analogies help to convey characters' arguments.

How does Shakespeare use imagery to explore themes or create mood?

- Sensory images add emotional impact, e.g. Portia's extended tactile metaphor of mercy as **'gentle rain'** falling **'from heaven'**.

- Ideas such as fortune and hope are exemplified by images of ships, storms and sea voyages.

- Mood is created by rich language, as in Lorenzo and Jessica's references to the night in Act V Scene 1, or the descriptions of the caskets.

How does Shakespeare use imagery to construct character?

- Characterisation is enhanced by powerful imagery, e.g. Morocco boasts of how he would **'Pluck the young sucking cubs from the she-bear'**.

- Simile and metaphor indicate characterisation, e.g. Antonio calls himself a **'tainted wether of the flock'** and Shylock is described as a wolf by Gratiano.

How does Shakespeare use symbolism?

- Lead, silver and gold caskets represent ideas about truth, vanity and value.
- Belmont symbolises a world of fairy-tale allusions and princely quests.
- Portia's and Nerissa's rings symbolise the unifying ending of the play which brings together lovers and wealth.
- Gratiano refers to Greek philosopher Pythagoras's belief that **'souls of animals infuse themselves/Into ... men'** in comparing Shylock to a wolf.

Five key quotations

1. Imagery – Gratiano's warning about young love: 'With overweather'd ribs and ragged sails,/Lean, rent, and beggar'd by the strumpet wind!' (II.6.19–20)

2. Simile – Antonio: 'An evil soul producing holy witness/Is like …/A goodly apple rotten at the heart.' (I.3.94–6)

3. Metaphor – Gratiano to Shylock: 'thy desires/Are wolfish, bloody, starv'd, and ravenous' (IV.1.137–8)

4. Morocco on the symbolism of fairy-tale Belmont: 'the vasty wilds/Of wide Arabia are throughfares now/For princes to come view fair Portia' (II.7.41–3)

5. Religious allusions – Shylock on Jacob from the Bible: 'he was blest;/And thrift is blessing if men steal it not.' (I.3.84–5)

Note it!

Shakespeare's imagery takes the audience beyond Venice and Belmont to picture the seas where Antonio's ships founder, or the Genoa market-place where Jessica sells her mother's ring for a monkey.

Exam focus

How can I write about Shakespeare's use of imagery? AO2

You can explore how imagery enhances characterisation.

Throughout the play, Shylock is associated with wolves and dogs, generally as a term of abuse used by others. In the court-room scene, Gratiano calls Shylock 'wolfish, bloody, starv'd, and ravenous'. These adjectives create an image of Shylock as inhuman and desperate for blood – Antonio's. But, Shylock himself earlier argued he has been treated like a dog, so it follows that he now behaves like an animal.	Overall point about imagery
	Evidence
	Analysis of language use
	Makes link to imagery earlier in play

Now you try!

Finish this paragraph about the use of simile to develop a theme. Use one of the quotations from the list.

Shakespeare develops the theme of appearance and reality through the use of imagery in Antonio's observation..

LANGUAGE Dramatic techniques

Five key things about Shakespeare's use of dramatic techniques

1. He **creates contrasts** in pace, action and setting between **Belmont** and **Venice**, and **different** types of **street**, **judicial** and **domestic** scenes.
2. **Information** is **revealed** slowly to ratchet up **dramatic tension**.
3. Shakespeare uses a **distinctive** voice for particular characters, e.g. Shylock's rhetorical questions, Lancelot's tumbling prose.
4. Juxtaposition of **situations**, **characters** and **relationships** is used to create interesting ideas or plot lines.
5. He moves between the comic and the tragic to sustain **audience interest**.

How does Shakespeare use contrast to sustain interest?

- Short, active street scenes in Venice contrast with more set-piece rituals involving the casket test in Belmont.
- Relationships are contrasted through action: e.g. Shylock's anger with Jessica and Portia's father's care for her future.
- Comedy is used for light relief: Lancelot's trickery and the ring plot link, nevertheless, to key themes.

How does Shakespeare use distinctive dramatic voices?

- Shylock's language is characterised by rhetorical appeals to other characters and the audience (**'Hath not a Jew eyes?'**) and short bursts of anger.
- Morocco, Arragon and Bassanio are all given long, thoughtful speeches that cast light on their character.
- Portia's character is established by her initial complaints about being restricted by her father's will, humorous observations about her suitors, courtly love speech to Bassanio and powerful rhetoric in the trial scene.

How does Shakespeare use time and action dramatically?

- The play takes place over approximately three months, but interest and tension is sustained by switching from Venice to Belmont – and drawing out the Prince of Morocco's arrival.
- Foreshadowing through gradual release of information creates dramatic irony – e.g. Shylock's initial aside about getting revenge on Antonio.

Five key quotations

1. Scenes of action – Jessica to Lorenzo: 'I will make fast the doors, and gild myself/With some moe ducats, and be with you straight.' (II.6.50–1)

2. Dramatic tension – Salarino: 'in the Narrow Seas that part/The French and English, there miscarried/A vessel' (II.8.29–31)

3. Distinctive voice – Shylock: 'Hath not a Jew eyes? Hath not a Jew hands, organs, dimensions, senses, affections, passions?' (III.1.52–3)

4. Juxtaposition – Gratiano to Bassanio: 'You saw the mistress, I beheld the maid./You lov'd, I lov'd' (III.2.198–9)

5. Conventions of tragedy – Antonio: 'Say how I lov'd you, speak me fair in death' (IV.1.273)

Note it!

Try to visualise the action on stage. For example, how close does Shylock come to cutting away the pound of flesh? While not stated directly in the script, productions often show Shylock sharpening the blade, indicating how far Shakespeare wanted to build suspense.

Exam focus

How can I write about Shakespeare's use of voice? (AO2)

You can discuss how main characters speak in particular ways.

Shakespeare deliberately gives characters distinctive voices. For example, Shylock's language, especially when	Overall point about voice
he talks about suffering or revenge, is characterised by rhetorical questions and appeals. 'Hath not a Jew	Specific example
eyes?' he asks in Act III Scene 1, and then emphasises the point by rhetorically repeating the phrase, 'Hath	Analysis of language use
not …?'. This has a strong emotional impact on the audience who would find it difficult to disagree.	Effect of language

Now you try!

Finish this paragraph about the use of contrast. Use one of the quotations from the list.

Shakespeare uses contrast in pace to maintain audience interest, for example in Act II Scene 6 when Jessica quickly throws ....

EXAM PRACTICE Understanding the exam

Five key things about the exam

1. You will have **one** question on *The Merchant of Venice* which will be based on a **passage** given to you on the exam paper.
2. It will focus on **Shakespeare's presentation** of an aspect of the play, such as a **character**, a **relationship** or a **theme**.
3. You will have about **45–50 minutes** to read and respond to the question.
4. The question is worth **30 marks**.
5. The question assesses **AOs 1, 2 and 3, with an extra 4 marks for AO4**. Remember that **AO3** relates to **context**.

What will a question look like?

	You must refer to the given passage
1. Starting with this extract, explore how Shakespeare presents Portia as an independent character. Write about:	You must explain the techniques Shakespeare uses
● how Shakespeare presents Portia as independent in this extract	This is the area you must tackle
● how Shakespeare presents Portia as independent in the play as a whole. **[30 marks] AO4 [4 marks]**	A reminder to begin with the given extract
	A reminder to **also** write about the whole of the play

Do all questions look the same?

● Not all questions will begin this way. Some might contain statements you must argue for or against. For example, **'Shakespeare's presentation of Venice shows it to be male-dominated.' Starting with this extract, explore how far you agree with this opinion.**

● Not all questions will be about a single character. Some might ask you about a **relationship** between two characters, e.g. between Portia and Bassanio.

What do I need to do to get a good mark?

Use this grid to understand what your current level is and how to improve it:

	AO1 Read, understand, respond	**AO2** Analyse language, form, structure and effects	**AO3** Show understanding of contexts
High	• You make **precise references** to the **passage** and *The Merchant of Venice* **as a whole**. • Your argument is **well-structured**, with quotations **fluently embedded** in sentences. • You cover **both** the extract and the whole play.	• You **analyse** and **interpret** the methods Shakespeare uses **very effectively**. • You **explore thoughtfully** the effects of these on the reader. • You show **excellent use** of subject terminology.	• You make **detailed, relevant links** between specific elements of the play and social and historical contexts.
Mid	• You make a **range of references** to the passage and the play as a whole. • You respond in **a clear, logical way** with **relevant** quotations chosen.	• You **explain clearly** some of the methods Shakespeare uses, and **some effects** on the reader. • You use **mostly relevant** subject terminology.	• You show **clear evidence** of understanding context which is **linked** to the play in places.
Lower	• You make **some references** to the passage and play as a whole, but in rather a **patchy** way. • You make **some useful points** but evidence is **not always clear or relevant**.	• You make **occasional attempts** to explain Shakespeare's methods but these are a little **unclear**. • You show **some use** of subject terminology.	• You demonstrate **basic awareness** of context but **links** to the play are **undeveloped** and **not always relevant**.

 AO4 You can gain up to 4 marks for **AO4**, which assesses your use of spelling, punctuation and grammar. For top marks: use a **range** of vocabulary and sentence structures, adopt a **clear, purposeful and effective** writing style, and make sure your spelling and punctuation are **accurate**.

EXAM PRACTICE Character questions

Read this exam-style character question

Read the following extract from Act I Scene 1 of *The Merchant of Venice* and then answer the question that follows.

At this point in the play Bassanio is talking to his friend, a merchant called Antonio.

> **ANTONIO**
> Well, tell me now what lady is the same
> To whom you swore a secret pilgrimage,
> That you to-day promised to tell me of?
> **BASSANIO**
> 'Tis not unknown to you, Antonio,
> 5 How much I have disabled mine estate,
> By something showing a more swelling port
> Than my faint means would grant continuance.
> Nor do I now make moan to be abridg'd
> From such a noble rate, but my chief care
> 10 Is to come fairly off from the great debts
> Wherein my time, something too prodigal,
> Hath left me gag'd. To you, Antonio,
> I owe the most in money and in love,
> And from your love I have a warranty
> 15 To unburden all my plots and purposes
> How to get clear of all the debts I owe.
> **ANTONIO**
> I pray you, good Bassanio, let me know it,
> And if it stand as you yourself still do
> Within the eye of honour, be assur'd
> 20 My purse, my person, my extremest means
> Lie all unlock'd to your occasions.

2. Starting with this moment in the play, explore how Shakespeare presents Antonio as a good friend to Bassanio. Write about:

● how Shakespeare presents Antonio as a good friend in this scene
● how Shakespeare presents Antonio as a good friend in the play as a whole.

[30 marks] AO4 [4 marks]

NOW read this further character question

Read this passage from Act IV Scene 1 and answer the question that follows. In this scene, Antonio is facing death after failing to repay his debt to Shylock.

> **ANTONIO**
> I pray you think you question with the Jew.
> You may as well go stand upon the beach
> And bid the main flood bate his usual height;
> You may as well use question with the wolf
> 5 Why he hath made the ewe bleat for the lamb;
> You may as well forbid the mountain pines
> To wag their high tops and to make no noise
> When they are fretten with the gusts of heaven;
> You may as well do anything most hard,
> 10 As seek to soften that – than which what's harder? –
> His Jewish heart. Therefore I do beseech you
> Make no more offers, use no farther means,
> But with all brief and plain conveniency
> Let me have judgment, and the Jew his will.
> **BASSANIO**
> 15 For thy three thousand ducats here is six.
> **SHYLOCK**
> If every ducat in six thousand ducats
> Were in six parts, and every part a ducat,
> I would not draw them; I would have my bond.
> **DUKE**
> How shalt thou hope for mercy, rendering none?
> **SHYLOCK**
> 20 What judgment shall I dread, doing no wrong?

3. 'Shakespeare presents Shylock as a vengeful figure.'

Starting with this extract, explore how far you agree with this statement.

Write about:

● how Shakespeare presents Shylock as vengeful in this scene
● how Shakespeare presents Shylock as vengeful in the play as a whole.

[30 marks] AO4 [4 marks]

EXAM PRACTICE Planning your character response

Five key stages to follow

1. **Read** the **question**; **highlight** the key words.
2. **Read** the **extract** with the **key words** from the **question** in mind.
3. Quickly **generate ideas** for your response.
4. **Plan** for paragraphs.
5. **Write** your response; **check it** against your plan as you progress.

What do I focus on?

Highlight the **key words**:

2. Starting with this moment in the play, explore how Shakespeare presents Antonio as a good friend to Bassanio. Write about:
   - how Shakespeare presents Antonio as a good friend to Bassanio in this scene
   - how Shakespeare presents Antonio as a good friend to Bassanio in the play as a whole. **[30 marks] AO4 [4 marks]**

What do they tell you? Focus on both extract and whole text; explain what specific methods are used; stick to topic – Antonio as a friend to Bassanio.

How should I read the passage?

- Check for any immediate links to the question (e.g. Bassanio admits Antonio has already helped him out more than anyone else).
- Look for any evidence/quotations you could highlight (e.g. **'To you, Antonio,/I owe the most in money and in love'**).

How do I get my ideas?

Note your ideas in a spider diagram or list them in a table:

The extract

Bassanio is able to discuss his problems with him

Antonio has lent him money before

Antonio's friendship

The play as a whole

Antonio allows Bassanio to use his good name

He repeatedly asks for their love/friendship to be remembered when he dies

The extract	The play as a whole
● Bassanio is able to discuss his problems with him	● Antonio allows Bassanio to use his good name
● Antonio has lent him money before	● He repeatedly asks to be remembered when he dies

How do I structure my ideas?

Make a **plan** for **paragraphs**.* Decide the order for your points:

● Paragraph 1: *In the extract, they share intimate plans – 'secret pilgrimage' to win Portia. Also, Bassanio's debts, etc. are 'not unknown' to Antonio.*

● Paragraph 2: *Bassanio is open about spending his inheritance ('disabled mine estate') and owing money – yet Antonio willingly offers to help him.*

● Paragraph 3: *Antonio does not have money to hand and is prepared to make a bargain with Shylock to help Bassanio, despite the latter's misgivings ('fair terms and a villain's mind').*

● Paragraph 4: *Antonio refuses to plead for mercy; he sees himself as weak ('tainted wether of the flock'); at least Bassanio profits even if he dies.*

● Paragraph 5: *In Act IV Scene 1, Antonio asks to be remembered as a true friend to Bassanio – this seems to override all other emotions.*

How do I write effectively?

Write **clear**, **analytical** paragraphs and **embed** your evidence fluently, e.g.

In the extract, Shakespeare presents the intimate relationship between the two men. Bassanio has clearly already talked with Antonio about his 'secret pilgrimage' to win Portia. The word 'secret' suggests he has only shared this with Antonio, implying his trust. Indeed, other friends in the group – Gratiano, Salarino, etc. – have all left the stage, recognising the strong bond between the two. As Bassanio states, his impoverished situation is 'not unknown' to Antonio.	Overview point – extract
	Evidence fluently embedded
	Language analysis
	Link back to earlier in scene
	Summary point with additional quotation

Now you try!

Re-read Question 3 on page 65 and plan your response in the same way.

* The plan above and the sample answers on pages 68 and 70 have five paragraphs, but you don't need to be limited to this if you have more points to include.

What does a Grade 5 answer look like?

Read the task again, then the sample answer below.

2. Starting with this moment in the play, explore how Shakespeare presents Antonio as a good friend to Bassanio.

Write about:

- how Shakespeare presents Antonio as a good friend in this scene
- how Shakespeare presents Antonio as a good friend in the play as a whole.

[30 marks] AO4 [4marks]

In this extract, Bassanio wants to talk about his plans to Antonio and Antonio is happy to listen. They must have talked about things before as Antonio says Bassanio had 'promised to tell me of' some 'lady'. Clearly if Bassanio is willing to talk about secrets and love then Antonio must be a good friend. It was not unusual for male friendship sometimes to be valued even more highly than between men and women in Shakespeare's day, and in the play this sometimes seems to be the case.

Bassanio's speech would probably put other friends off. He goes on about how he has 'disabled' his estate, meaning lost his fortune and how he owes Antonio 'the most in money and in love'. Using a superlative like 'most' tells us that Bassanio owes more to Antonio than anyone else. Yet at the end Antonio makes it clear he will willingly lend more to him and that his 'purse, my person, my extremest means' are fully open to him. He hasn't even heard what Bassanio wants so this shows how good a friend he is.

Later in Act I Scene 3 we find out what Antonio is prepared to do for Bassanio. He is prepared to borrow money for him from Shylock, someone he despises and hates. It is a big deal because of their different views on money and life. It makes Bassanio suspicious. 'I like not fair terms and a villain's mind.' But Antonio agrees to a bond which is potentially dangerous.

AO1 Introduces focus well

AO1 Suitable quotation

AO3 Relevant context about gender theme

AO4 Too informal

AO2 Good language analysis

AO1 Neatly sums up point

AO1 Important quotation but undeveloped

It is maybe no surprise when Antonio's ships fail as sea trade would have been very risky in Shakespeare's time. This may be why Antonio accepts his fate without ever blaming Bassanio. His letter to Bassanio in Act III Scene 2 states: 'all debts are cleared between you and I if I might but see you at my death.' All he wants as he says in the next scene is for Bassanio to come, 'to see me pay his debt, and then I care not.' This shows the extent of his feelings of friendship for Bassanio.

Paragraph 4

When Antonio is about to face death in Act IV Scene 1, he gives a final speech in which he asks Bassanio not to 'grieve' for him; he doesn't want Bassanio to feel bad. He even says he will pay his debt with 'all my heart' which is a bit of a gruesome joke, but also means he is very happy to do it. Bassanio's response that he would even lose his wife and his own life suggests that he recognises how good a friend Antonio has been.

Paragraph 5

Check the skills

Re-read paragraphs four and five of this response and:

- highlight other **points** made
- circle any reference to **context**
- underline any places where the student has made an **interpretation**.

Now you try!

Look again at paragraph three (*'Later in Act I Scene 3 …'*, etc.) and improve it by:

- Adding a **reference to the context of Jewish/Christian conflict**
- **Explaining** the effect of Bassanio's comment about a 'villain's mind'
- Ending with a more detailed **summary point** about the risks Antonio is taking
- Improving the overall **style** by making sure your sentences **flow**; using **connectives** to **link** ideas

What does a Grade 7+ answer look like?

Read the task again, then the sample answer below.

2. Starting with this moment in the play, explore how Shakespeare presents Antonio as a good friend to Bassanio.

Write about:

- how Shakespeare presents Antonio as a good friend in this scene
- how Shakespeare presents Antonio as a good friend in the play as a whole.

[30 marks] AO4 [4 marks]

In the extract, Shakespeare presents the intimate relationship between the two men. Bassanio has already talked with Antonio about his 'secret pilgrimage' to win Portia. The word 'secret' suggests he has only shared this with Antonio, implying his trust. Indeed, prior to this, Gratiano, Salarino and others have all left the stage, acknowledging the strong bond between the two. As Bassanio states, his impoverished situation is 'not unknown' to Antonio.

> **AO1** General point introduces key perspective

> **AO2** Detailed language analysis

The extent of Antonio's friendship is also indicated by Bassanio's admission that he already owes him the 'most in money and in love.' Bassanio implicitly links his own behaviour to that of the 'prodigal' son who in the Bible was forgiven by his father, despite having wasted all the money given to him. This suggests that Antonio, too, has a father's love for Bassanio, willing to accept his faults and even to further support him where others might have been more circumspect. Such love will put him in huge danger.

> **AO3** Relevant link to literary context

> **AO4** Fluent expression

At the end of the extract, Antonio pledges to unlock his 'person' and 'extremest means' to help Bassanio, and we soon find out this is not just words. In Act I Scene 3, it is his person in the 'pound of flesh' contract that is placed in 'extreme' danger – although he does not realise it at this point. Bassanio suspects it and states that he doesn't approve of 'fair terms and a villain's mind', but Antonio's friendship blinds him to the warning. That he is willing to put aside religious and business prejudice for his friend is telling.

> **AO1** Developed argument with apt evidence

> **AO1** Thoughtful insight into motives

When Antonio's trading ventures appear to fail, he continues to act as father of a prodigal son. Far from blaming Bassanio, his letter to him in Act III Scene 2 states 'all debts are cleared between you and I', which is both a private and public way to stress his support, provided Bassanio sees him before he dies. Indeed, he adds that once this is done, 'then I care not.' This demonstrates the depths of male friendship in Shakespeare's time, which were often viewed as more profound even than heterosexual ones.

— Paragraph 4

There is debate about why Antonio seems so willing to accept death. As a somewhat isolated figure, it seems his relationship with Bassanio is especially deep, so much so that he begs Bassanio not to 'grieve' for him or to feel guilt. He adds that he will pay his debt 'with all my heart', which can be taken both literally as he loses a pound of flesh and metaphorically – giving his life just as Bassanio starts a new one with Portia. Bassanio responds saying he would sacrifice his wife and 'all the world' in recognition of how good a friend Antonio has been. Interestingly, though, it is Antonio who in reality stands to lose everything, not Bassanio, which may suggest the friendship is more one-sided than we think.

— Paragraph 5

Check the skills

Re-read paragraphs four and five of this response and:

- identify any particularly **fluent** or **well-expressed** ideas
- find any further references to **Shakespeare's language and techniques**
- highlight any places where the student has shown **deeper insight** and offered **original** or particularly **thoughtful** ideas or made interesting **links**.

Now you try!

Now, using the plan you made for Question 3 on page 67, write a full response. Here's a reminder of the question:

3. 'Shakespeare presents Shylock as a vengeful figure.' Starting with this extract, explore how far you agree with this statement. Write about:

- how Shakespeare presents Shylock as vengeful in this scene
- how Shakespeare presents Shylock as vengeful in the play as a whole.

[30 marks] AO4 [4 marks]

- Try to match your answer to the High Level objectives on page 63.

Read this exam-style theme question

Read the following extract from Act III Scene 3 of *The Merchant of Venice* and then answer the question that follows.

At this point in the play Antonio has been arrested and is on his way to prison.

> **ANTONIO**
>   Let him alone.
> I'll follow him no more with bootless prayers.
> He seeks my life, his reason well I know:
> I oft deliver'd from his forfeitures
> 5 Many that have at times made moan to me;
> Therefore he hates me.
> **SOLANIO**
>   I am sure the duke
> Will never grant this forfeiture to hold.
> **ANTONIO**
> The duke cannot deny the course of law;
> For the commodity that strangers have
> 10 With us in Venice, if it be denied,
> Will much impeach the justice of the state,
> Since that the trade and profit of the city
> Consisteth of all nations. Therefore go.
> These griefs and losses have so bated me
> 15 That I shall hardly spare a pound of flesh
> Tomorrow to my bloody creditor.
> Well, jailer, on. Pray God Bassanio come
> To see me pay his debt, and then I care not.   [*Exeunt*]

4. Starting with this extract, explore how Shakespeare presents ideas about justice and the law in the play.

Write about:

- how Shakespeare presents justice and the law in this extract
- how Shakespeare presents justice and the law in the play as a whole.

[30 marks] AO4 [4 marks]

Read this extract from Act II Scene 8 of *The Merchant of Venice* and then answer the question that follows.

At this point in the play Antonio's friends are reporting Shylock's response to his daughter's elopement.

> **SOLANIO**
> The villain Jew with outcries rais'd the duke,
> Who went with him to search Bassanio's ship.
> **SALARINO**
> He came too late, the ship was under sail.
> But there the duke was given to understand
> 5 That in a gondola were seen together
> Lorenzo and his amorous Jessica.
> Besides, Antonio certified the duke
> They were not with Bassanio in his ship.
> **SOLANIO**
> I never heard a passion so confus'd,
> 10 So strange, outrageous, and so variable,
> As the dog Jew did utter in the streets:
> 'My daughter! O my ducats! O my daughter!
> Fled with a Christian! O my Christian ducats!
> Justice! The law! My ducats and my daughter!
> 15 A sealed bag, two sealed bags of ducats,
> Of double ducats, stolen from me by my daughter!
> And jewels – two stones, two rich and precious stones,
> Stolen by my daughter! Justice! Find the girl!
> She hath the stones upon her and the ducats.'
> **SALARINO**
> 20 Why, all the boys in Venice follow him,
> Crying his stones, his daughter, and his ducats.
> **SOLANIO**
> Let good Antonio look he keep his day,
> Or he shall pay for this.

5. Starting with this extract, explore how Shakespeare presents the theme of prejudice in the play. Write about:

- how Shakespeare presents the theme of prejudice in this extract
- how Shakespeare presents the theme of prejudice in the play as a whole. **[30 marks] AO4 [4 marks]**

Five key stages to follow

1. **Read** the **question**; **highlight** key words.
2. **Read** the **extract** with the **key words** from the **question** in mind.
3. Quickly **generate ideas** for your response.
4. **Plan** for paragraphs.
5. **Write** your response; **check it** against your plan as you progress.

What do I focus on?

Highlight the **key words**:

4. Starting with this extract, explore how Shakespeare presents ideas about justice and the law in the play. Write about:
   - how Shakespeare presents justice and the law in this extract
   - how Shakespeare presents justice and the law in the play as a whole.

   [30 marks] AO4 [4 marks]

What do they tell you? Focus on both extract and whole text; explain what specific methods Shakespeare uses; stick to justice and the law as the main topic.

How should I read the passage?

- Check for any immediate links to the question (e.g. Antonio's arrest, effect on Venice if law not followed).
- Look for any evidence/quotations you could highlight (e.g. **'The duke cannot deny the course of law'**).

How do I get my ideas?

Note your ideas in a spider diagram or list them in a table:

The extract		The play as a whole
Friends' feelings – duke won't allow the 'pound of flesh' payment	**Justice and the law**	*Shylock's feelings – he has been unjustly treated & duke 'shall grant me justice'*
Status of Venice – law must be followed for its business reputation		*The way the law is turned against Shylock to defeat him*

The extract	The play as a whole
● *Solanio believes that the duke will see inhumanity of Shylock's case* ● *Global reputation of Venice will suffer if justice 'be denied'*	● *Shylock believes in natural justice after Antonio's treatment of him* ● *Portia turns justice against him: 'The Jew shall have all justice'*

How do I structure my ideas?

Make a **plan** for **paragraphs**.* Decide the order for your points:

● Paragraph 1: *In the extract Antonio refuses to seek further release from the bond or Shylock's hold over him.*

● Paragraph 2: *Antonio says the case must be upheld because Venice's reputation will be damaged 'if it be denied'.*

● Paragraph 3: *Elsewhere (e.g. in the trial), the duke is shown as powerless to intervene due to Venice's reputation.*

● Paragraph 4: *Shylock's sense of justice is linked to revenge, but he uses the law to achieve it.*

● Paragraph 5: *Ultimately, Portia uses the law to defeat Shylock, while claiming he will 'have all justice'. It could be argued that he does not get justice, given his treatment: is the law different for some?*

How do I write effectively?

Write **clear**, **analytical** paragraphs and **embed** your evidence fluently, e.g.

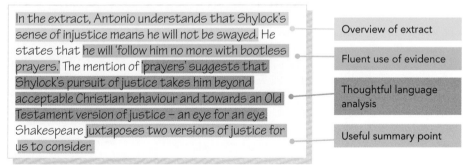

In the extract, Antonio understands that Shylock's sense of injustice means he will not be swayed. He states that he will 'follow him no more with bootless prayers.' The mention of 'prayers' suggests that Shylock's pursuit of justice takes him beyond acceptable Christian behaviour and towards an Old Testament version of justice – an eye for an eye. Shakespeare juxtaposes two versions of justice for us to consider.

- Overview of extract
- Fluent use of evidence
- Thoughtful language analysis
- Useful summary point

Now you try!

Re-read Question 5 on page 73 and plan your response in the same way.

*The plan above and the sample answers on pages 76 and 78 have five paragraphs, but you don't need to be limited to this if you have more points to include.

What does a Grade 5 answer look like?

Read the task again, then the sample answer below.

4. Starting with this extract, explore how Shakespeare presents ideas about justice and the law in the play.

Write about:

● how Shakespeare presents justice and the law in this extract

● how Shakespeare presents justice and the law in the play as a whole.

[30 marks] AO4 [4 marks]

In the extract, Antonio is being led away by a jailer. Clearly, the law is being used against him and there is little he can do, despite his friends' best efforts. He tells his friends, 'Let him alone', meaning don't bother trying to change Shylock's mind. Antonio clearly knows Shylock wants him to pay with his life and will use the law to get his 'pound of flesh'. This is because Shylock felt unjustly treated and didn't like how Antonio rescued people in debt to him, or the general attitude to Jews in Venice.

> **AO1** Clear understanding of overall situation

> **AO1** Relevant quotation

Shakespeare makes an important point about Venice and the law in this extract. Antonio knows how important Venice is in trade and business, and talks about the 'commodity that strangers have/With us in Venice', and how this can't be damaged by the duke changing the laws just to suit someone who is powerful or respected like him. 'Commodity' means privilege, so it means people wouldn't choose Venice as a place to do business. So it doesn't really matter what is right, business comes first, even if the law seems unjust towards Antonio.

> **AO3** Makes historical context link

> **AO2** Clearly explained language point

> **AO2** Structural point, if rather basic

Justice has been important from the start of the play. In Act I Scene 3 when Shylock meets Antonio he describes how Antonio has mistreated him: 'You call me … cut-throat dog,/And spit upon my Jewish gaberdine'. This is bound to have an effect on the audience, even in Shakespeare's time, when Jews in England were not treated well. But we can probably guess Shylock is going to use the law to get back at Antonio.

> **AO3** Historical context, but needs development

> **AO4** Vocabulary is too informal

In the trial scene, Shylock uses the law to force the duke to accept Shylock's right to his 'pound of flesh'. He says, 'If you deny it, let the danger light/Upon your charter and your city's freedom!' By using the word 'danger' he appears to threaten the duke, saying no one will trust Venice's law, so it could be said he and Antonio agree on that point at least. Venice was one of the most important trading centres in the world so he is probably right in that respect.

Paragraph 4

However, ultimately Shakespeare shows that there is a way to retain Venice's reputation and use the law against Shylock. Portia allows Shylock to believe he is about to have his bond before she stops him. By this time a different law – about seeking the life of a Christian – is used to defeat him. He loses everything and is forced to give his lands and property to Lorenzo and Jessica when he dies. The duke says 'I pardon thee' so Shylock is not executed but is left with nothing. Maybe the decision is fair, maybe it isn't, but it shows that the law, even in Venice, can be twisted.

Paragraph 5

Check the skills

Re-read paragraphs four and five of this response and:

- highlight other **points** made
- circle any reference to **context**
- underline any places where the student has made an **interpretation**.

Now you try!

Look again at paragraph three ('*Justice has been important ...*', etc.) and improve it by:

- **Analysing** what the effect of the insult about Shylock would be on the audience
- **Explaining** how Jews in England were mistreated
- Adding a **reference or quotation** from Act I Scene 3 that explains Shylock's plans
- Improving the overall **style** by making sure your sentences **flow**; using **connectives** to **link** ideas

What does a Grade 7+ answer look like?

Read the task again, then the sample answer below.

4. Starting with this extract, explore how Shakespeare presents ideas about justice and the law in the play.

Write about:

- how Shakespeare presents justice and the law in this extract
- how Shakespeare presents justice and the law in the play as a whole.

[30 marks] AO4 [4 marks]

In the extract and the play as a whole, Shakespeare presents justice as an idea which has both domestic and political ramifications. In deciding not to plead further with Shylock with 'bootless prayers', Antonio implies that personal enmity between them can lead only one way – to the Old Testament, an eye for an eye, idea of justice which will triumph over forgiveness. However, there is more at stake here: Antonio is aware that the law of Venice is also in the dock, and in sacrificing himself for his friend, he is also sacrificing himself for the continued success of his city.

AO1 Confident synthesis of argument

AO2 Insight into language

AO1 Fluent link to additional idea

Here, Antonio dismisses Solanio's comments that the duke must intervene to save his life. The law must take precedence and the duke 'cannot deny it'. If traders from 'all nations' are to trust in the 'commodity' Venice offers then they need to know that the state can be trusted. As perhaps the most powerful trading centre in the world at the time, Venice would have had rivals, such as Genoa, only too willing to label the city corrupt.

AO4 Fluent short sentence

AO3 Very well-developed contextual point

Law and justice have, until now, been of a purely personal nature. Shylock's treatment, as he outlined it in Act I Scene 3, suggested that in normal circumstances natural justice should hold sway. Many, even in Shakespeare's England, which had seen no Jews since their exclusion in 1290, would have felt some sympathy for the money-lender when spat upon and treated like a 'dog'. But as the play progresses, Shylock's appeal to the law shows he is willing to corrupt justice to feed the 'ancient grudge' he has referred to.

AO1 Key point expressed succinctly

AO3 Additional contextual point

AO2 Excellent interpretation of language

Yet, like Antonio, Shylock understands Venice's law. At the start of Act IV Scene 1 he errs by threatening the duke with it. If the duke doesn't allow him his bond, he warns, 'let the danger light/ Upon your charter and your city's freedom!' Threatening the Venetian city-state's independence is a risky move. Perhaps the way in which Portia and the duke combine to throw his justice back at him is as much a punishment for a Jew over-reaching himself, setting himself as higher than the state and, of course, God.

— Paragraph 4

The justice Shylock receives at the end of the play may come from the state, but it wounds him personally. It is bad enough that his money should go to Antonio; but worse still that his inheritance should pass to the Christian who ran off with his daughter. 'I am not well' claims Shylock as he is about to leave the stage. Even then the law follows him as his last line indicates, 'Send the deed after me/And I will sign it.' Relentless justice will pursue him even after the play has finished.

— Paragraph 5

Check the skills

Re-read paragraphs four and five of this response and:

● identify any particularly **fluent** or **well-expressed** ideas

● find any further references to **context**

● highlight any places where the student has shown **deeper insight** and offered **original** or particularly **thoughtful** ideas or made interesting **links**.

Now you try!

Now, using the plan you made for Question 5 on page 75, write a full response. Here's a reminder of the question:

5. Starting with this extract, explore how Shakespeare presents the theme of prejudice in the play.

Write about:

● how Shakespeare presents the theme of prejudice in this extract

● how Shakespeare presents the theme of prejudice in the play as a whole.

[30 marks] AO4 [4 marks]

● Try to match your answer to the High Level objectives on page 63.

Now you try!

Now, apply the skills you have learned to these two new questions:

- Note down key points from the extract.
- Select the key quotations you want to use from the extract.
- Repeat the process with other ideas from the play as a whole.
- Write your answer.
- Look at the suggested list of key points in the **Answers** (page 88).

Read this extract from Act IV Scene 1 of *The Merchant of Venice* and then answer the question that follows.

In this scene, Antonio faces death at the hands of Shylock.

> **ANTONIO**
> Commend me to your honourable wife.
> Tell her the process of Antonio's end,
> Say how I lov'd you, speak me fair in death,
> And when the tale is told, bid her be judge
> 5 Whether Bassanio had not once a love.
> Repent but you that you shall lose your friend
> And he repents not that he pays your debt.
> For if the Jew do cut but deep enough
> I'll pay it instantly with all my heart.
> **BASSANIO**
> 10 Antonio, I am married to a wife
> Which is as dear to me as life itself;
> But life itself, my wife, and all the world,
> Are not with me esteem'd above thy life.
> I would lose all, ay, sacrifice them all
> 15 Here to this devil, to deliver you.
> **PORTIA**
> Your wife would give you little thanks for that
> If she were by to hear you make the offer.

6. Starting with this extract, explore how the relationship of Bassanio and Portia is presented. Write about:

- how Shakespeare presents their relationship in this extract
- how Shakespeare presents their relationship in the play as a whole.

[30 marks] AO4 [4 marks]

Read this extract from Act II Scene 7 of *The Merchant of Venice* and then answer the question that follows.

In this scene, Morocco reads the scroll contained inside the gold casket.

> **MOROCCO**
>   O hell! What have we here?
> A carrion death, within whose empty eye
> There is a written scroll. I'll read the writing.
>   'All that glitters is not gold;
> 5   Often have you heard that told.
>   Many a man his life hath sold
>   But my outside to behold.
>   Gilded tombs do worms infold.
>   Had you been as wise as bold,
> 10   Young in limbs, in judgement old,
>   Your answer had not been inscroll'd.
>   Fare you well, your suit is cold.'
> Cold indeed, and labour lost;
> Then farewell heat, and welcome frost.
> 15 Portia, adieu; I have too griev'd a heart
> To take a tedious leave: thus losers part.
>
>   [*Exit* Morocco *with his train*
>
> **PORTIA**
> A gentle riddance! Draw the curtains, go.
> Let all of his complexion choose me so.   [*Exeunt*

7. Starting with this extract, explore how Shakespeare presents ideas about outward appearance and inner reality.

Write about:

● how appearance and reality is presented in this extract

● how appearance and reality is presented in the play as a whole.

[30 marks] AO4 [4 marks]

GLOSSARY

Literary or language term	Explanation
allusion	an indirect reference to something else
analogy	a comparison between one thing and another
antagonist	character in a story whose objective is to challenge or defeat the hero
aside	something said by a character, which is intended to be heard by the audience but not by the characters on stage
commedia dell'arte	Italian style of comedy popular between the 16th and 18th centuries featuring stock characters or types
dialogue	a conversation between two or more characters; the words spoken by a character
dramatic irony	when the audience can see more significance in the words of a character than the characters in the play can
foreshadowing	a hint of what is to come in a work of poetry, fiction or drama
image	vivid picture created in the audience's mind
in media res	literally, 'in the middle of things' – refers to stories that begin in the heart of the action
juxtaposition	two ideas, images or objects positioned close together to highlight their differences
lyrical	having a 'song-like' tone, often expressing ideas about beauty
metaphor	when one thing is used to describe another to create a striking or unusual image
mood	feeling or atmosphere

Literary or language term	Explanation
motif	an image, idea or situation that recurs throughout the text, forming a pattern
pace	speed
prose	a form of language that has the natural flow of speech, rather than poetry, which has a rhythmic structure
protagonist	the main or a major character
rhetorical question	a question asked for effect rather than for an answer
set piece	something that is designed in an elaborate/ conventional way to create an impressive effect
setting	the place or environment where the events in a story take place
simile	when one thing is compared directly with another using 'like' or 'as'
stereotype	fixed or over-simplified idea about a person or place
subplot	a secondary storyline that supports the main one, often by reinforcing the theme
symbol	something that represents or suggests an idea, belief or action, e.g. a dove as a symbol of peace
theme	key idea or issue arising from the play's action and language
tone	the particular attitude or mood expressed in language
trope	a significant or recurrent idea or theme
voice	the particular manner of speaking or narration

ANSWERS

Note that the sample paragraphs given here provide only one possible approach to each task. Many other approaches would also be valid and appropriate.

PLOT AND STRUCTURE

Act I Scenes 1 and 2 – Now you try! (page 5)
From his first words in the play, Antonio is presented as someone who struggles emotionally and cannot understand why he is 'so sad.' This impression is further developed when he states that 'I have much ado to know myself' – meaning it takes a great deal of trouble for him to even work out his own actions. Throughout the play there is a continuing mystery as to what sort of person Antonio is.

Act I Scene 3 – Now you try! (page 7)
We are given clues about the danger Shylock poses for Antonio in Bassanio's comment that he likes 'not fair terms and a villain's mind'. Clearly Bassanio mistrusts the deal Shylock is offering. The balance created in Shakespeare's line between the opposing phrases 'fair terms' and 'villain's mind' reinforces the strength of Bassanio's feelings.

Act II Scenes 1–5 – Now you try! (page 9)
The theme of prejudice is developed when Morocco enters the play and his first words to Portia are 'Mislike me not for my complexion'. This suggests he knows the racial prejudice that already exists in this powerful Christian society. Later he is perhaps proved right after he fails the casket test and Portia states, 'Let all of his complexion choose me so.'

Act II Scenes 6–9 – Now you try! (page 11)
Shakespeare provides hints of Antonio's later difficulties when Salarino reports that a 'vessel of our country richly fraught' has sunk. He does not mention whether it is one of Antonio's, but Salarino's mind immediately turns to Antonio, knowing his ships are at risk, and knowing they, too, are carrying precious cargo. This is bound to make an audience wonder whether Antonio's fortunes will also be sunk.

Act III – Now you try! (page 13)
As the act opens, Antonio's friends report the possible loss of his ships and, by the end, Antonio confirms this when he says in his letter that 'ships have all miscarried' and admits his bond 'is forfeit'. The sudden reality of this situation is presented in stark, short phrases and is a hammer blow after Jessica's escape and Bassanio and Portia's happiness. The tension is suddenly developed as Shylock's 'merry sport' becomes a fatal possibility.

Act IV – Now you try! (page 15)
Shylock is presented as absolutely set on revenge in this scene, as Antonio's comparison demonstrates: 'You may as well use question with the wolf/Why he hath made

the ewe bleat for the lamb'. In other words, Shylock is like a bloodthirsty wolf, whose nature it is to murder the innocent lamb. This comparison of Shylock with beasts emphasises his inhuman pursuit of revenge.

Act V – Now you try! (page 17)
The humorous mood is created by Portia's joke to Bassanio, telling him that in revenge she'll take him for her 'bedfellow', which the audience realises simply means that she'll sleep with herself. This clever playing around with the situation lightens the mood after the high drama of the court-room scene.

Form and structure – Now you try! (page 19)
The Jessica/Lorenzo love subplot benefits the play in a number of ways: firstly, by paralleling the developing relationship of Portia and Bassanio, and secondly as a potential model for how Christians and Jews may live in harmony. However, the reality is that rather than 'end this strife' as Jessica hopes, it heightens Shylock's anger and hatred of Christians, particularly Antonio.

Quick revision – Quick quiz (page 20)
1. Venice. 2. He is sad. 3. To woo Portia. 4. Her dead father. 5. 3000 ducats. 6. Lancelot. 7. Gold and jewels. 8. Gold. 9. A ship has sunk in the English Channel which might be his. 10. The Prince of Arragon. 11. Tubal. 12. A ring. 13. A letter arrives. 14. They are going to disguise themselves and follow him to Venice. 15. The duke. 16. Balthazar. 17. Any blood. 18. Execution. 19. Bassanio's ring. 20. Three of his ships have returned safely.

Quick revision – Power paragraphs (page 21)
1. The two main plots are Shylock's revenge, and Bassanio's wooing of Portia. These are brought together because Bassanio's need for money causes Antonio to depend on Shylock, who hates him. Two of the themes of these plots are brought together too, as Bassanio states – 'To you, Antonio,/I owe the most in money and in love'.
2. Act IV, set in a Venice courtroom, represents the dramatic climax of the play with emotions laid bare. This is shown in the depth of Shylock's hate, and Bassanio's love for Antonio, whom he prizes as much as 'life itself, my wife, and all the world'. In contrast, Act V which opens on a starry night in Belmont, is calming and ultimately light-hearted as the couples reunite and the ring trick is revealed.

Quick revision – Exam practice (page 21)
- This scene sets the tone for a very different type of story from that in Scene 1 – Nerissa's description of 'chests of gold, silver, and lead' immediately brings to mind fairy tales and myths, which contrasts with the everyday reality of money and trade. It will also be important in bringing Bassanio to Belmont, and it is as a result of the casket test that Portia gets to learn about the danger Antonio is in.

- The lottery is important in developing the theme of father/child relationships; Nerissa says that 'holy men at their death have good inspirations', recognising Portia's late father's wish for his daughter to be happy. The lottery also links with the idea of fortune through the risks Antonio is taking – whether his ships will return safely.

SETTING AND CONTEXT

Jewish and Christian society – Now you try! (page 23)
The issue of lending or accumulating money is central to the play, as is shown when Shylock mentions how 'many a time and oft' Antonio has criticised him for lending money for interest. This suggests that they have regularly crossed paths and that business has been a point of conflict for some time. Their mutual dislike began in the Rialto, the business centre of Venice.

Settings – Now you try! (page 25)
Shakespeare introduces the setting of Belmont through Bassanio's description of travellers flocking to see Portia as they would the 'golden fleece'. This links her and her home to the myth of Jason and his quest for the golden fleece and elevates Bassanio's quest into something noble.

Quick revision – Quick quiz (page 27)
1. They were baptised into the Christian faith. 2. 1290. 3. Barabas. 4. A Portuguese Jew, a doctor to Queen Elizabeth I. 5. Fair or beautiful hill. 6. The Rialto. 7. Genoa. 8. Her wealth, home and land. 9. He set the casket test as part of his will. 10. She wins Antonio's freedom in the court-room scene.

Quick revision – Power paragraphs (page 27)
a) The setting of Belmont – 'beautiful hill' – is presented as a separate, almost fairy-tale place. This implies Portia is like a princess worth winning, both in beauty and in personal qualities. But it could equally be described as a sort of prison for Portia, and she needs to escape from it to fully demonstrate her intelligence and independence.
b) Venice is where a number of friendships are shown, from those of Lorenzo, Gratiano and Salarino to the more specific friendships of Bassanio and Antonio. It is also used to show the friendship between Shylock and Tubal, who lends Shylock the cash for the loan and later reports on Jessica's behaviour in Genoa. We trace the development of Antonio and Bassanio's friendship from Bassanio's original request for money. Antonio tells Bassanio to 'Try what my credit can in Venice do' – giving him permission to borrow money on his reputation. Later, the friendship is shown at its most profound – almost a form of love – when Antonio accepts his fate and death, and asks Bassanio not to grieve for him.

CHARACTERS

Shylock – Now you try! (page 29)
Shakespeare emphasises the dislike for Shylock when Antonio states that he would be 'as like …/To spit on

thee again' when Shylock challenges his treatment of him. The fact that Antonio admits how he has treated Shylock shows the contempt shown for Shylock by the Christian business community, and may alter our perception of Shylock.

Antonio – Now you try! (page 31)
Shakespeare presents Antonio's understanding of how Venice operates when he states that 'The duke cannot deny the course of law'. In accepting the bond he has signed, he recognises, as a businessman, that Venice's trading reputation would be damaged if it was shown to be unreliable. Viewing Antonio positively, this could fit with his opinion of Shylock's business practices being corrupt, for example in charging interest.

Bassanio – Now you try! (page 33)
Shakespeare shows that Bassanio feels deeply about the impact of his actions on his closest friend. When he receives the letter from Antonio in Act 3 Scene 2 which states that his friend is facing death, Bassanio calls 'every word in it a gaping wound'. It is as if he is physically and emotionally injured by what might happen to Antonio.

Portia – Now you try! (page 35)
Shakespeare reveals that Portia, while showing independent thought, also thinks of herself as innocent and unworldly. For example, in accepting Bassanio as her future husband she says she is an 'unlesson'd girl'. This may refer to her virtue, and it certainly seems strange to think of her as an obedient, quiet wife when we see evidence of her witty intelligence.

Gratiano and Nerissa – Now you try! (page 37)
One of Nerissa's core functions in the play is to act as a confidante and adviser to Portia. When Portia is frustrated by the casket test set by her father which she thinks restricts her freedom, Nerissa consoles her, saying her 'father was ever virtuous' and that the test was a clever idea. This proves that Nerissa is a good judge of character, as Portia ultimately meets Bassanio through the test.

Lorenzo and Jessica – Now you try! (page 39)
In Act V Scene 1, when Lorenzo refers to himself as Jessica's 'unthrift love', as they wait for Portia and Bassanio to return, he makes it clear he has little money. What money he and Jessica took from Shylock is apparently gone, so he is lucky that he will inherit from Shylock on his death. Lorenzo is another character who benefits from Portia's skill in the courtroom.

The princes – Now you try! (page 41)
Morocco has several functions, one of which is to bring a different world into the play through reference to places such as the 'vasty wilds/Of wild Arabia'. Even more importantly it also raises Portia's status as a sort of fairy princess worth winning by these princes who have travelled from foreign lands.

ANSWERS

Quick revision – Quick quiz (page 42)
1. Bassanio. 2. Gratiano. 3. As 'a scholar and a soldier'. 4. She describes her suitors wittily; she is also witty in devising the ring trick. 5. Antonio lent money with no interest. 6. Antonio has spat at him, called him names, etc. 7. He seems reluctant because ships are risky ventures. 8. Tubal. 9. He mistrusts the 'fair terms and a villain's mind.' – in other words it seems too good to be true. 10. It demonstrates his vanity. 11. The Prince of Morocco. 12. His own foolish head and the one depicted in the silver casket. 13. She sold her mother's ring, suggesting a lack of respect or love. 14. He is influenced by outside appearances. 15. She entrusts the house to Jessica and Lorenzo. 16. A ring. 17. She will become a Christian. 18. He speaks to him angrily and violently. 19. He compares himself to 'a tainted wether of the flock' (a sick lamb/sheep). 20. Both dress up, take on a traditionally male role, give a ring, trick their partner and get married.

Quick revision – Power paragraphs (page 43)
1. Antonio seems resigned to his fate in that he accepts the rule of law and that the duke can't bend the rules for him. However, he also seems to consider himself unworthy of life, calling himself 'a tainted wether of the flock', a sick lamb that does not have the strength to continue. This seems to fit with his earlier comments about being melancholy.
2. As Portia's companion, Nerissa listens while Portia lists the unsuitable men who have come to woo her, but more importantly, she talks good sense, advising Portia that the casket test was an intelligent choice of her father's. She herself is lively, and in the ring trick makes fun of Gratiano saying that 'the doctor's clerk … did lie with me'. She is, of course, the clerk, showing she is able to hold her own when it comes to tricking the men.

Quick revision – Exam practice (page 43)
• Bassanio is worried about Gratiano's 'skipping spirit' which he is concerned might damage his hopes with Portia. The word 'skipping' suggests Gratiano is loud and energetic, which does not really fit with a visit to woo someone Bassanio wants to marry, and who is perhaps still in mourning for her dead father.
• Gratiano's response shows that he understands how he needs to behave, but the humorous way he replies, saying he will 'Wear prayer books' and 'sigh and say "Amen"' is rather mocking of religious behaviour, and suggests he doesn't necessarily take Bassanio's concerns seriously. He also says he will only 'swear but now and then', suggesting he won't be able to entirely curb his personality.

THEMES

Prejudice – Now you try! (page 45)
References in the play to Shylock's behaviour that confirm anti-Semitic stereotypes include Solanio's report of how angry Shylock is at Jessica's disappearance when he comments on Shylock's complaint that 'She hath the stones upon her and the ducats!'. This emphasis on the material value of what he has lost fits with ideas about Jewish greed and sharp practice.

Money and commerce – Now you try! (page 47)
Shakespeare shows that trade and commerce are bound up with risk, notably when Bassanio refers to the 'merchant-marring rocks' which Antonio's ships appear to have hit. Given that Antonio has no cash to hand to lend Bassanio, this is a very precarious situation to be in with all his 'ventures' tied up in his ships carrying cargo around the world.

Love and friendship – Now you try! (page 49)
Shakespeare shows that male friendship can be powerful as Bassanio's declaration that he 'would lose all, ay, sacrifice them all' for Antonio, when Antonio faces death, implies that he would lose his wife and his possessions, to save him. This mirrors the fact that Antonio has sacrificed all for Bassanio – and one could argue that giving your life for a friend is more powerful than marrying for love.

Revenge and justice – Now you try! (page 51)
Shakespeare shows that Shylock is already thinking about revenge early in the play as when he first sees Antonio he immediately considers how to 'catch him once upon the hip', meaning at a disadvantage. This is particularly ironic as it also refers to a part of the body, which is how Shylock will ultimately try to hurt him. The 'ancient grudge' Shylock feels, also suggests he has been thinking of revenge for a long time.

Appearance and reality – Now you try! (page 53)
Shakespeare shows how false information can mask the truth when Bassanio questions Salerio. The audience needs to believe Antonio's cargo ships have really sunk, so Bassanio's comment 'What, not one hit?' meaning not one success, seems to be evidence that Antonio is fatally threatened. This of course turns out not to be the case – as in the final scene, we learn that three of Antonio's ships have 'richly come to harbour suddenly'.

Fathers and children – Now you try! (page 55)
Shakespeare shows that Portia's father knew his child better than Shylock does Jessica. For example, Portia's dead father seems to have devised a means of trapping her in Belmont, without independent choice, but as Nerissa says, he was 'ever virtuous' so clearly wanted the best for her. Even if the casket test is a lottery, it seems that Portia ends up with a man she loves, so perhaps her father was a good judge of character.

Quick revision – Quick quiz (page 56)
1. It was probably the most important trading centre in the world at the time. 2. Antonio doesn't charge interest, which brings down the rate Shylock can charge. 3. Ships. 4. He wins the wealth of Portia. 5. Three from: Portia/Nerissa, Bassanio/Gratiano, Jessica/Lancelot, Antonio/Bassanio. 6. Self-love or

vanity. 7. She gives up family and her Jewish faith.
8. Bassanio. 9. Mercy, forgiveness. 10. Because of
Antonio's business dealings, and his vocal and physical
abuse. 11. Jessica's elopement, taking his jewels and
money with her. 12. He demands the letter of the law,
but this specifies only flesh, no blood, and as a result he
loses everything. 13. She is a young woman who has
recently pledged her heart, body, wealth and property
to a man – Bassanio – suggesting she has little power
and yet she wields power in the courtroom. 14. He will
seek 'revenge'. 15. Jessica, Portia, Nerissa. 16. Neither
the silver or gold caskets contain the image of Portia;
it is contained within 'ugly lead'. 17. It appears he has
lost all his money, but in fact at the end of the play it is
reported that three of his ships have come into port full
with rich cargo. 18. He sets a casket test to determine
who her future husband will be. 19. He tells him that he
is dead! 20. A 'wise' one.

Quick revision – Power paragraphs (page 57)

1. Portia tells him he is gaining the 'full sum of me',
which in her terms means someone who is innocent
and virtuous – unblemished by the world. However,
the use of the word 'sum' is apt as Bassanio is
gaining much more. He will also become master of
'this house, these servants' and of everything that
belongs to her. He will gain possession of her as a
person and of her literal possessions.
2. While Portia's father, in devising the casket test,
seems to know her better than she knows herself,
Shylock was unaware of Jessica's plans to leave.
The anger in 'I would my daughter were dead at
my foot' suggests it was a complete shock to him
– that there was little common ground between
them before that. The fact that she runs off with a
Christian shows how far they had become divided.

Quick revision – Exam practice (page 57)

- Shakespeare presents justice firstly as related to the
reputation of the city of Venice. Shylock threatens
the duke by stating that if he 'deny it, let the danger
light/Upon your charter and your city's freedom'. He
seems to be saying that if he, as a businessman in
the city, does not get justice then who will want to
trade with Venice or trust the deals that are made
there?
- Shylock also indicates that the sort of justice he wants
is very much his decision. If he chooses not to be paid
back in money but prefers to be paid with Antonio's
death, that is his 'humour' (wish). He doesn't even
repeat the ways that Antonio has mistreated him, and
simply states that he bears Antonio a 'lodg'd hate
and a certain loathing'. This is personal.

LANGUAGE

Imagery and symbolism – Now you try! (page 59)

Shakespeare develops the theme of appearance
and reality through the use of imagery in Antonio's
observation that 'An evil soul producing holy witness/
Is like …/A goodly apple rotten at the heart.' The
simile of a fruit rotting from the inside is a powerful

way to describe the hatred Shylock feels for Antonio.
It also reflects Antonio's strong feelings about Shylock
quoting the Bible to support his business practices.

Dramatic techniques – Now you try! (page 61)

Shakespeare uses contrast in pace to maintain
audience interest, for example in Act II Scene 6 when
Jessica throws caskets to Lorenzo in the street below,
telling him she'll 'make fast the doors' before she races
off to steal more ducats. In contrast, the next scene
inside Portia's house in Belmont is slow and deliberate,
as the Prince of Morocco draws 'aside the curtains' to
reveal the caskets, as everyone stands and watches.

EXAM PRACTICE

Planning your character response – Now you try! (page 67)

- **Paragraph 1**: Go straight into your first point: In the
extract, Antonio uses a series of powerful analogies
to indicate the depth of Shylock's vengeful nature,
comparing him to the tide, the wolf and powerful
wind, 'the gusts of heaven'.
- **Paragraph 2**: Shylock confirms this view of him by
refusing double the loan payment, and even stating
that he'd reject six times double the amount.
- **Paragraph 3**: Shylock's vengeful nature is shown
from the first time he sees Antonio in Act I Scene 3,
when he immediately plans to 'catch him … upon
the hip'.
- **Paragraph 4**: His angry language at various other
moments (e.g. when Jessica leaves him) also
conveys his desire for revenge.
- **Paragraph 5**: In Act IV Scene 1, Shylock rejects
all calls for mercy, all further offers of money,
and refuses anything that might lessen Antonio's
suffering.

Grade 5 sample answer – Check the skills (page 69)

Points: Paragraph 4: may be why Antonio accepts
his fate without ever blaming Bassanio. Paragraph 5:
When Antonio is about to face death in Act IV
Scene 1, he gives a speech in which he asks Bassanio
not to 'grieve' for him; he doesn't want him to feel bad.
Context: Paragraph 4: sea trade would have been
very risky in Shakespeare's time.
Interpretation: Paragraph 5: Bassanio's response that
he would even lose his wife and his own life suggests
that he recognises how good a friend Antonio has
been.

Grade 5 sample answer – Now you try! (page 69)

Later in Act I Scene 3 we find out what Antonio is
prepared to do for Bassanio. He will borrow money
for him from Shylock, someone he despises and hates
partly due to the tensions between Christians and
Jews which were a reality of the time. This is a key
issue as these differences were not only religious but
related to business. This is why Bassanio suspects the
'fair terms and a villain's mind', a motif of appearance
masking reality which we see throughout the play.
Antonio is putting himself in danger in three ways. He
is lending to a friend who has been unreliable; he is

borrowing from a known enemy; and his own shipping business is not without risk.

Grade 7+ sample answer - Check the skills (page 71)

Fluent/well-expressed ideas: Paragraph 4: Concise opening sentence: When Antonio's ventures appear to fail, he continues to act as father of a prodigal son. Paragraph 5: Complex idea expressed well: A somewhat isolated figure, it seems his relationship with Bassanio is especially deep, so much so that he begs Bassanio not to 'grieve' for him or to feel guilt. **Language and techniques**: Paragraph 4: his letter to him in Act III Scene 2 states 'all debts are cleared between you and I', which is both a private and public way to stress his support. Paragraph 5: He adds that he will pay his debt 'with all my heart', which can be taken both literally as he loses a pound of flesh and metaphorically. **Deeper insight**: Paragraph 5: There is debate about why Antonio seems so willing to accept death. As a somewhat isolated figure, it seems his relationship with Bassanio is especially deep, so much so that he begs Bassanio not to 'grieve' for him or to feel guilt.

Grade 7+ sample answer - Now you try! (page 71)

AO1
- In the extract, Antonio describes the depths of Shylock's vengeance through a range of analogies to the natural world.
- Shylock, in the extract, rejects any form of loan repayment, however much is offered.
- In Act I Scene 3, Shylock immediately thinks of revenge when he meets with Antonio.
- In Act IV Scene 1, he is impervious to appeals for mercy, for money or to relieve Antonio's suffering.

AO2
- In the extract, Antonio's analogies link Shylock's vengeful nature to the violent appetite of wolves, and the power of nature.
- The juxtaposition of Shylock's response to the duke's request has an argumentative logic to it. He echoes the duke's question.
- Elsewhere, Shylock's short, repetitive assertion of 'I will have my bond' or 'let him look to his bond' indicates his obsessive pursuit of revenge.
- In Act IV Scene 1, the analogies of Shylock to a wolf are repeated with Gratiano calling him 'wolfish' and 'ravenous'.

AO3
- The idea of vengeance – 'an eye for an eye', as in the Old Testament of the Bible – is linked to Shylock's idea of justice which contrasts with the Christian view (as Portia argues) of forgiveness.
- The conflict between Jews and Christians in the play is linked to different interpretations of the Bible stories, and to the stereotypical view of Jews' avarice – lending money for interest. Shylock's revenge is partly driven by Antonio affecting his business.

Planning your theme response - Now you try! (page 75)

Paragraph 1: In the extract, the unpleasant ways in which Solanio and Salarino talk about Shylock fit with the

way other Christians talk about him elsewhere in the play. **Paragraph 2**: The language they use ('villain', 'dog') and the way they seem to enjoy his anger (calling it 'So strange, outrageous'), show their prejudice. They also mention the children who mock him. **Paragraph 3**: Prejudice is also shown in the way Shylock claims in Act I Scene 1 to have been treated by Antonio in the past and is implied in other speeches he makes ('Hath not a Jew eyes?'). **Paragraph 4**: Prejudice could also be seen in the way his relationship with Jessica is portrayed – with him as a controlling, insensitive father. Also in the final trial scene when the justice he gets from the Christian court means that he justice everything. **Paragraph 5**: There is other prejudice in the play in the way Morocco is presented and the mockery of Portia's suitors, perhaps demonstrating English views of outsiders at the time.

Grade 5 sample answer - Check the skills (page 77)

Points: Paragraph 4: Shylock uses the law to force the duke to accept Shylock's right to his 'pound of flesh'. Paragraph 5: Shakespeare shows that there is way to retain Venice's reputation and use the law against Shylock. **Context**: Paragraph 4: Venice was one of the most important trading centres in the world so he is probably right in that respect. **Interpretation**: Paragraph 4: so it could be said he and Antonio agree on that point at least. Paragraph 5: Maybe the decision is fair, maybe it isn't, but it shows that the law, even in Venice, can be twisted.

Grade 5 sample answer - Now you try! (page 77)

Justice has been important from Act I Scene 3 when Shylock describes how Antonio has called him 'cut-throat dog' and would 'spit upon my Jewish gaberdine'. This is bound to create audience sympathy, even in Shakespeare's time, when Jews in England were not really seen (they had been expelled in 1290) or were viewed as dangerous (Elizabeth's doctor was executed for allegedly trying to poison her). So it is hardly surprising that Shylock uses the law to gain his revenge, as seen in his keenness to get Antonio to meet him immediately at the 'notary' to seal the bond.

Grade 7+ sample answer - Check the skills (page 79)

Fluent ideas: Paragraph 4: Yet, like Antonio, Shylock understands Venice's law. At the start of Act IV Scene 1 he errs in threatening the duke with it. Paragraph 5: The justice Shylock receives at the end of the play may come from the state, but it wounds him personally. **Context**: Paragraph 4: Threatening the Venetian city-state's independence is a risky move. Paragraph 5: but more still that his inheritance should pass to the Christian who ran off with his daughter. **Deeper insight**: Paragraph 4: perhaps the way in which Portia and the duke combine to throw his justice back at him is as much a punishment for a Jew over-reaching himself, setting himself as higher than the state and, of course, God. Paragraph 5: Even then the law follows him as his actual last line indicates, 'Send the deed after me/And I will sign it.' Relentless justice will pursue him even after the play has finished.

Grade 7+ sample answer – Now you try! (page 79)
AO1

- The attitudes of Christians to Shylock in this extract and elsewhere show prejudice both in the language used to describe him, and in the actions towards him.
- In this extract, Solanio and Salarino mock how Shylock reacts to Jessica leaving him, reporting his concern with his money as much as his daughter's betrayal.
- Elsewhere in the play, Shylock describes how Antonio has abused him verbally and physically (in Act I Scene 3) and how he has damaged Shylock's business practice. The justice he receives at the end of the play could be viewed as biased.
- Other forms of prejudice exist in the way Morocco is presented, and in Portia's mockery of her other suitors.

AO2

- The noun phrases 'villain Jew' and 'dog Jew', as well as the description of Shylock's understandable anger as 'So strange, outrageous', show Salarino and Solanio's view of him.
- The repetition of 'ducats' and the link made to religion ('Christian ducats') suggests Shylock's objections to Jessica leaving are related more to his faith and his greed, than losing a daughter.
- Shylock's speech in Act I Scene 3 links with this in that Antonio called him 'cut-throat dog'. Later, Gratiano uses similar bestial analogies to describe Shylock as 'wolfish' and 'ravenous' (Act IV Scene 1).
- The Prince of Morocco anticipates Portia's view of him by telling her 'Mislike me not for my complexion' at the start of Act II Scene 1, but when he leaves in Act II Scene 7, Shakespeare suggests with Portia's line ('Let all of his complexion choose me so') that she has her own prejudices.

AO3

- The stereotypical view in Elizabethan times of the avaricious, alien Jew is represented in Solanio's description of Shylock.
- Stereotypes prevalent in Shakespeare's day about other nations are represented by the presentation of Morocco.

Practice questions – Question 6 (page 80)
AO1

- In the extract, Bassanio claims his relationship with Portia is all-important but then places Antonio's worth above hers.
- Portia (in the guise of Balthazar) wrily observes this would not be welcomed by her 'If she were by'.
- Bassanio and Portia are seen as already in love at the start of Act III Scene 2, and are very anxious about the casket test, fearing he might fail.
- Portia willingly gives her life over to Bassanio once he chooses correctly, but later shows she retains independence through the ring trick. Bassanio does not attempt to deceive her, showing his basic decency.

AO2

- The heightened drama of the trial scene shows the extent of Bassanio's closeness to Antonio – 'I would lose all, ay, sacrifice them all' he says of Portia and his possessions.
- Dramatic irony is strong in Portia's reply that his wife 'would give you little thanks'. She seems to be reminding him of his main duties as husband.
- In Act III Scene 2, Bassanio uses the image of a man tortured – 'I live upon the rack' to express his desperation to be with Portia.
- In Act V Scene 1, Bassanio's language ('Pardon this fault', 'forgive me') suggests he values Portia and hopes his actions will be seen as honourable.

AO3

- Portia's speech in Act III Scene 2 when she verbally gives herself and her possessions to Bassanio is a reflection of reality in Elizabethan times rather than a mark of weakness.
- The trope of disguise is one common to many Shakespeare plays as a way of establishing the true relationship between lovers.

Practice questions – Question 7 (page 81)
AO1

- In the extract, the gold casket contains a lifeless skull. The message in the casket is a rhyme that contains a lesson for Morocco and for the audience that not everything that shines on the outside is actually precious.
- Elsewhere in the play, Shylock's seeming willingness to enter into a 'merry sport' with Antonio hides his hatred and plans for revenge. Jessica manages to conceal her plans to leave Shylock (disguised as a boy).
- Other characters disguise themselves for a range of reasons: Lancelot to have fun with his father; Portia to become a male lawyer.
- Disguise is both an instrument of hate and prejudice, and one of justice and lighter comedy.

AO2

- The alliterative, riddle-like, 'All that glisters is not gold' is a memorable metaphor for relationships and situations in the play.
- The powerful image of a decorous tomb which has worms within it reminds the audience of mortality but also to beware false gods – judge people on their deeds, not their appearance.
- Ironically, Antonio, in Act I Scene 3, comments on the need to judge carefully in his simile likening a 'villain with a smiling cheek' to 'A goodly apple rotten at the heart'.
- Justice is shown to be something that can trick and deceive: Bassanio says in Act III Scene 2: 'what plea so tainted and corrupt/But, being season'd with a gracious voice,/Obscures the show of evil?' – this could be describing Shylock's offer of friendship in Act I Scene 3.

AO3

- The disguising of reality in the form of the casket riddle and as a plot device link Belmont to fairy-tale challenges and trickery.
- Christian ideas of justice may have been convenient ways to hide prejudice in Elizabethan times.